Advent

LET EVERY HEART PREPARE HIM ROOM

by Kerry van der Vinne

Copyright © 2022 Ambry Press
All rights reserved

No part of this publication may be reproduced, stored in a retrieval system, or transmitted, in any form or in any means – by electronic, mechanical, photocopying, recording or otherwise – without prior written permission.

Scripture is cited from several translations:

THE HOLY BIBLE, NEW INTERNATIONAL VERSION®, NIV®
Copyright © 1973, 1978, 1984, 2011 by Biblica, Inc.™
Used by permission. All rights reserved worldwide.

The King James Version of the Bible is in the public domain.

(All scripture is quoted from the NIV, unless noted as KJV).

Traditional materials reproduced in the "resource" section of this book are in the public domain:

The Book of Common Prayer

Hymn Texts: Come, Thou Long Expected Jesus (Charles Wesley, 1707-88); Come, Thou Redeemer of the Earth (attr. Ambrose of Milan, 4th century); Creator of the Stars of Night (Anon., 7th century); Gabriel's Message (Sabine Baring-Gould, 1834-1924); Hark! A Herald Voice is Calling (Anon., 6th century); Jesus Came, The Heavens Adoring (Godfrey Thring, 1823-1903); Jesus Christ, The Apple Tree (Anon., 18th century); Lo, He Comes, With Clouds Descending (Charles Wesley, 1707-88); O Come, Divine Messiah! (Simon J. Pellegrin, 1663-1745); O Come, O Come, Emmanuel (tr. John Mason Neale, 1818-66); O Heavenly Word, Eternal Light (Anon., 6th century); On Jordan's Bank, The Baptist's Cry (Charles Coffin, 18th century); Rejoice, All Ye Believers (Laurentius Laurenti, 1660-1722); The Advent of our God (Charles Coffin, 18th century); The Linden Tree Carol (Anon., 15th century); The Lord Will Come And Not Be Slow (John Milton, 1608-74); The Truth Sent From Above (Anon./Traditional, collected in 1911); 'Thy Kingdom Come,' On Bended Knee (Frederick Lucian Hosmer, 1840-1929); Tomorrow Shall Be My Dancing Day (Anon./Traditional, collected in 1833); Wake, O Wake! With Tidings Thrilling (Philipp Nicolai, 16th century)

Advent Prose (c. 4th century)

O Antiphons (c. 6th century)

Nine Lessons and Carols (originally published/inaugurated in 1880)

ISBN: 978-1-990425 14-1 (paperback)
ISBN: 978-1-990425-15-8 (e-book)

Table of Contents

INTRODUCTION

Let Every Heart Prepare Him Room

This book is an invitation. If you've ever been troubled by the superficial consumerism surrounding the season—if you've ever felt out of sync with the festive cheer—if you've ever wondered whether there might be *more* to Advent—then this invitation is for you.

For many of us, the month of December is characterised by frantic activity and heightened emotion as we anticipate Christmas with shopping, decorating, cooking, and a flurry of seasonal obligations. Even those among us who love the bustle and cheer can be overwhelmed. Meanwhile, what has happened to Advent? In the frenzy to "get ready" for the outward rituals of Christmas, we can fail to prepare our *hearts*. This book is an invitation to step away from the tumult, if only for a brief time each day, to do just that.

The season can also be a difficult one for other reasons. Grief, family estrangement, financial strain, loneliness, disappointment, anxiety—whatever burdens we carry, they can crowd in at this time of year and make us want nothing more than to skip the month of December entirely. In an effort to avoid painful associations, we can inadvertently overlook a season that is especially in tune with the broken-hearted, a season that is uniquely equipped to usher us into the presence of our loving Saviour. This book is an invitation to look more deeply at the Advent message of hope and love—to be reminded that Jesus came for sick and needy sinners like you and me.

It's not always obvious from the way we observe it in modern times, but Advent was actually designed to be a season of quiet, prayerful reflection. Over many centuries, believers have marked the four weeks leading up to Christmas with prayers, readings, and music that focus not on the miracle of the incarnation itself, but on all that led up to the first coming of Jesus: the darkness of human need, the long years of waiting, the message of the forerunner, and all of the promises and prophecies that would be fulfilled in one perfect Saviour.

There is a profound relevance for us today in keeping the season of Advent as it was originally intended—because we too are awaiting the Messiah. We are waiting for his return, his second advent. Like the faithful believers of the Old Testament, we know what it is to grapple with darkness, and to feel exhausted with waiting. Like them, we need the assurance of God's loving plan; we need to remember that he has kept his promises to past generations, and that we can also trust him to keep those promises that are yet to be fulfilled.

The message of Advent doesn't fit neatly into a soundbite or vignette. It's too complex, too deep, to compete with glitter and noise; and it's a hard sell in a culture that would rather skip straight to the big finish. But Advent is too important to be forgotten, because it is this season that prepares us to encounter our Lord. It is the spiritual journey of Advent which gives Christmas depth and power. If we want to celebrate a more meaningful "Christ-Mass," then we must prepare our hearts by participating in a more meaningful Advent.

Reclaiming Advent may seem like an impossible task. Where do we even begin? We begin with the simple step of making time and space for the journey. We begin by taking to heart the words of invitation that are spoken each year in a hushed candlelit chapel on Christmas Eve:

> Let us "prepare ourselves to hear again the message of the angels; in heart and mind to go even unto Bethlehem and see this thing which is come to pass... *Let us read and mark in holy scripture the tale of the loving purposes of God from the first days of our disobedience unto the glorious redemption brought us by this holy child*; and let us make this place glad with our carols of praise."[1]

Over the next four weeks, through a series of daily devotional readings, we'll follow this pattern of tracing our salvation-story through the pages of scripture. We'll also draw upon some beautiful lesser-known Advent texts that have been passed down through the centuries by our ancestors in the faith.

Are you willing to bear with some discipline in the weeks ahead—to let the presents remain under the tree until Christmas morning as it were? I promise it's worth the effort. So, set your alarm, dust off your hiking boots, and join with me in praying that this book will both encourage and challenge you along the Advent road, and that at the journey's end you'll find yourself entering into the joy of Christmas with fresh eyes and a spirit ablaze.

And now, let's take our first step down that road. The journey awaits.

---

[1] *These are the words of invitation given at the annual service of Nine Lessons and Carols. The full text is included in the resource section, page 154.*

Week One

OUT OF DARKNESS

The people walking in darkness
have seen a great light;
on those living in the land of deep darkness
a light has dawned.

ISAIAH 9:2

NOVEMBER 27

Remembering

As a father has compassion on his children,
so the Lord has compassion on those who fear him;
for he knows how we are formed,
he remembers that we are dust.

PSALM 103:13-14

What is *your* memory like? Is it sharp and detailed, like a photograph, even after many years have passed? Or does it soften and blur into something more like an impressionist painting? Most of us don't have to think very far back to be confronted by the limitations of our own memory—even of those things that we experienced ourselves.

God, on the other hand, has a very long memory. He remembers with perfect clarity all of the events of your life. He was at work when you were growing in the womb. He saw the generational patterns that would influence the home you were born into, woven over decades and centuries. And further back still, he was the one who breathed life into your first ancestor. There is no one who can know you and understand you as completely as he does.

Many within our world are having an identity crisis. They are looking for someone to tell them who they are—and there are plenty of answers vying to be believed—but the only true answer is found in hearing our own story, told by the one who really knows it, again and again, until we too know it by heart.

In many of the Old Testament psalms, we find a pattern of "recounting." The psalmists put into poetry the history of the people of God—what they had been through, and all that God had done for them. When the people repeated these psalms together, they were retelling their collective story, being reminded of who they were and to whom they belonged.

The memories weren't all good ones. There were photographs in the family album of ancient Israel that the psalmists must have been tempted to skip over. Isn't this true for all of us? We've all lived through chapters we'd rather forget. There have been sins, failures, and suffering. Sometimes remembering these things can feel like reopening a wound. We don't *want* to remember. In fact, we'd give a great deal to *forget*. But the recounting psalms have a lot to teach us, because they were not simply recitations of history. They were prayers and praises, designed to bring the whole of a people's experience into the presence of God, and in doing this, to gain a heavenly perspective on it all.

Consider Psalm 136. The opening verse says this:

> Give thanks to the Lord, for he is good.
> His love endures forever.

That second sentence—*"His love endures forever"*—is repeated 26 times throughout this psalm. Each verse begins with a snapshot from Israel's story, but closes with an acknowledgment of God's unchanging love. Their story took them into slavery in Egypt—but God's love endured forever. They wandered many years in the wilderness—still God's love endured forever.

Our stories, collective and individual, wherever they've taken us, have never been beyond God's reach. Even though we're the ones who have *lived* our stories, we don't have all the facts about them. God is the only one who knows all the hidden details. He is the one who can see our innate frailty, who can remember the dust we were made from. And his response to this? Compassion. Enduring love.

We're standing together on the threshold of Advent. This is a season that plunges us into the harsh light of remembering like no other. In order to prepare our hearts for the coming of Jesus, we must begin by remembering why his coming was needed—because without him we are hopelessly broken and forever separated from God. The journey of remembering will take us through some rough terrain, but we don't undertake this journey alone. We're in God's good hands. He is able to open our eyes to see how his enduring love has been constant, even in the worst moments of our lives. He has never been an indifferent observer, but rather a loving parent, ever-present, weeping, planning, sacrificing, following every heartbeat with unceasing interest. He is the one who has been there from the beginning, by our side through it all, and is even now leading us onwards to a glorious finale.

PRAYER & REFLECTION

* Set aside five minutes to sit in silence, reflecting on your spiritual need. It may be uncomfortable, but challenge yourself to stay with it. Close your time with this reminder: "Put your hope in the Lord, for with the Lord is unfailing love and with him is full redemption" (PSALM 130:7).
* One additional note: If there are unresolved chapters in your personal history that you'd rather forget, don't let them fester—examine them in the light of God's love, healing and forgiveness. Remember that if you're reading this right now, you *survived* those experiences. *His love endures forever.* It was true then. It is true now. It will be true whatever you face tomorrow.

NOVEMBER 28

A Dark Beginning

Now the earth was formless and empty, darkness was over the surface of the deep, and the Spirit of God was hovering over the waters.

GENESIS 1:2

Our world began in darkness. The opening sentences of Genesis tell us this much. All was formless and void. It was God's presence, his command, that brought light and life, order and fullness.

You probably know how the story progressed. God made everything good, but it did not *stay* good. Human beings chose disobedience, and in doing so turned away from the light of God's presence. Our world and our lives show the consequences of this all around: sin and death, illness and grief. The experience of "darkness" is universal and familiar. Our social media accounts may suggest otherwise, but we all know first-hand what it is to struggle, to feel lonely, empty, lost and hopeless. You and I are fallen people living in a dark world.

Light and darkness. This imagery is used throughout the Bible to convey something vital to our understanding of salvation. But because such imagery has sometimes been misapplied and twisted, causing great harm, it's important to note that this imagery was never meant to refer to pigment or hue. Soteriology has nothing to do with skintone.

Instead, light should make us think of warmth, growth and health. It's by light that we are able to see clearly. A place of light is one of innocence, hope and wholeness.

All of this describes the garden of Eden, humanity's first home. And it was *home* precisely because it was characterised by God's presence, and by an unbroken relationship with him. But that is not where we live.

Contrasted with this picture of light, we can better recognise what is meant by darkness. In the darkness, we *cannot* see clearly, we cannot move forward with confidence or hope, and the shame of our sin compels us to hide. The Bible has this to say about it:

> The way of the wicked is like deep darkness;
> they do not know what makes them stumble
> (PROVERBS 4:19).

> Everyone who does evil hates the light, and will not come into the light for fear that their deeds will be exposed (JOHN 3:20).

Darkness is what we get when we are separated from God. And yet there is good news, for God was—and is—not content to leave us in the dark. Throughout the Old Testament, the promise of darkness *dispelled* is repeated. The prophet Isaiah wrote:

> The people walking in darkness have seen a great light; on those living in the land of deep darkness a light has dawned (9:2).

With the privilege of hindsight, we know that these words pointed to Jesus, who was and is "the true light that gives light to everyone" (JOHN 1:9).

In a few short weeks we will celebrate the miracle of Christmas—a moment in human history when the light broke through our darkness. But we're in Advent now, and the season of Advent seeks to remind us that there is a *second* coming, and a *greater* dispelling of darkness, for which we still wait.

The traditional scripture readings[1] for the first Sunday

[1] *Further details can be found in the resource section, see pages 99 and 102.*

in Advent include this passage from Romans:

> The hour has already come for you to wake up from your slumber, because our salvation is nearer now than when we first believed. *The night is nearly over; the day is almost here* (13:11-12).

These verses were not addressed to Israel as it awaited the coming of the Messiah, but rather they are speaking to the Christian Church as it awaits his second coming. They are speaking to us, where we live, right now.

We live in a dark world. There's no sense in denying it. The night still surrounds us—but not for long. The light of Christ has come into the world, and he has given us hope. Salvation is very near. And though we cannot yet see clearly, the day is fast approaching when we shall.

PRAYER & REFLECTION

* Take a few minutes to consider if and how your life is burdened by the darkness of shame or despair. Invite God to bring the light of hope and forgiveness into these places. Slowly and contemplatively read Psalm 139 *(a shortened version is included below)*:

> You have searched me, Lord, and you know me. You know when I sit and when I rise; you perceive my thoughts from afar...
>
> If I say, "Surely the darkness will hide me and the light become night around me," even the darkness will not be dark to you; the night will shine like the day...
>
> For you created my inmost being; you knit me together in my mother's womb...
>
> Search me, God, and know my heart; test me and know my anxious thoughts. See if there is any offensive way in me, and lead me in the way everlasting.

NOVEMBER 29

Living in the Light

The hour has already come for you to wake up from your slumber, because our salvation is nearer now than when we first believed. The night is nearly over; the day is almost here. So let us put aside the deeds of darkness and put on the armour of light.

ROMANS 13:11-12

Does this passage sound familiar? It should, because we looked at it yesterday! But now I want to call your attention to the "so what" in this text. Wherever you see a word like "therefore" or "so," it's an indication that the author is about to come to a point, to tell readers why everything that's just been said matters.

The Apostle Paul, who wrote the letter to the Romans, has just finished telling us that change is afoot. Though the beginning of our story has been dark, the ending won't be. Jesus has come and made a way to heaven for us. He will come again to take us to that home. But in the meantime, we must be alert. In the meantime, we must "put aside the deeds of darkness" and "put on the armour of light." *We must lean towards our future, not our past.*

The Bible is pretty clear about what "the deeds of darkness" are. Romans 13 specifically mentions drunkenness, sexual immorality, debauchery, dissension, and jealousy. Elsewhere in scripture the "sin lists" identify greed, unwholesome talk, bitterness, rage, brawling, slander, and every form of malice. None of these lists are meant to be exhaustive, but each provides us with a series of potent snapshots. It's as if an instructor is holding them up to say, "See these? Your life *shouldn't* look like this." We can become overly familiar with these lists and pass over them with a feeling of self-righteousness—but we shouldn't. These letters were written to believers, like us, not so that they could pass judgement on others, but because no matter how many of these words we feel innocent of, there's always at least one we're tempted by or guilty of.

There's more to Paul's exhortation than a list of "do nots." The second part of his exhortation tells us what we *ought* to do—put on the armour of light. This is the armour that will equip us to overcome darkness and its deeds. Paul takes up the image of armour again and expands upon it in his letter to the Ephesians:

> Therefore put on the full armour of God, so that when the day of evil comes, you may be able to stand your ground, and after you have done everything, to stand. Stand firm then, with the belt of truth buckled around your waist, with the breastplate of righteousness in place, and with your feet fitted with the readiness that comes from the gospel of peace. In addition to all this, take up the shield of faith, with which you can extinguish all the flaming arrows of the evil one. Take the helmet of salvation and the sword of the Spirit, which is the word of God (6:13-17).

Living in the light requires that we equip ourselves with the armour that God provides. Darkness has characterised our past, and it continues to inhabit our present, but it is no longer who we are, and it is no longer how we should live.

We have the encouragement of knowing that our identity is in Christ and that we're citizens of a heavenly country. But being a bearer of light in a dark world also comes with responsibility. The lives we live here have purpose.

We are witnesses, pointing the world to the one who said, "I am the light of the world. Whoever follows me will never walk in darkness, but will have the light of life" (JOHN 8:12). And so we follow, and invite others to follow with us. And as we follow, our Father is transforming us, making us more like his beloved Son, more ready for an eternity without darkness.

PRAYER & REFLECTION

* Was your conscience "pricked" by the sin lists we looked at? Make your confession to the Lord, remembering that "if we confess our sins, he is faithful and just and will forgive us our sins and purify us from all unrighteousness" (1 JOHN 1:9).
* Reread Ephesians 6:13-17 *(previous page)*, noting those traits which act as spiritual armour. Ask for God's help in applying these protections in your own life.
* The "collect" (prayer) for the first Sunday of Advent[2] forms a meditation on the passage in Romans that we've been looking at, and focuses our attention on living faithfully as we await Jesus' return. Take some time to read slowly through the prayer—slowly enough to consider its words and add a few of your own:

  > Almighty God, give us grace that we may cast away the works of darkness, and put on the armour of light, now in the time of this mortal life, in which your son Jesus Christ came to visit us in great humility; that in the last day, when he shall come again in his glorious majesty, to judge both the living and the dead, we may rise to the life immortal; through him who lives and reigns with you and the Holy Spirit, now and ever. Amen.

---

[2] *Further details can be found in the resource section, see pages 99 and 102.*

NOVEMBER 30

Protoevangelium

Then the Lord God said to the woman, "What is this you have done?"

The woman said, "The serpent deceived me, and I ate."

So the Lord God said to the serpent, "Because you have done this, cursed are you above all livestock and all wild animals! You will crawl on your belly and you will eat dust all the days of your life. And I will put enmity between you and the woman, and between your offspring and hers; he will crush your head, and you will strike his heel."

GENESIS 3:13-15

The story in Genesis doesn't end with the glorious creation of a good world. The garden was contaminated by evil. Our human ancestors sinned against God by eating forbidden fruit. Spiritual darkness descended. There was a confrontation. Guilt, shame, and muddled confessions were swiftly followed by just judgement. And then, there was a prophecy. The natural consequences of disobedience would be devastating, echoing through the centuries, across the oceans and throughout our lives to this day. But even in that dark, distant moment, the light shone.

In the heart of this sad text lies a glimmer of hope. Theologians call it "the protoevangelium," which means "the first gospel." Read again verse 15, the words of God spoken to Satan in the serpent:

> I will put enmity between you and the woman, and between your offspring and hers; he will crush your head, and you will strike his heel.

It is there, at the very beginning, when sin destroyed human communion with God, that the promise of Jesus was first hinted at. One day, from the descendants of Eve, a child would be born with the power to destroy the work of the serpent and the curse of sin—though this would come with a price, a sacrifice.

*

One of the most beloved services that marks the celebration of Advent is called "Nine Lessons and Carols[3]." It is a very simple and beautiful service made up only of scripture readings ("lessons") interspersed with singing. The lessons are arranged to walk through the Old Testament story, beginning with the protoevangelium, tracing God's plan through the age of the patriarchs, noting the messianic visions of the prophets, and finally coming to those beloved gospel narratives that speak of God's promise fulfilled in the birth of Jesus Christ.

As we make our way through the season of Advent, we will touch upon many of these texts. Perhaps at first glance they will seem like disjointed fragments, but there is a thread that runs through these passages of scripture, connecting them all. As we continue on our journey we will see them come together to form a beautiful tapestry. At the farthest edge of the tapestry is the story of our dark beginnings, our fallenness, and those photos in the family album we'd rather forget. Running along the opposite edge is our identity as bearers of light in this dark world. But there's much more to see—and the thread connecting all of these things, illuminating them and making them unmistakably relevant is simply this: the love of God.

Return with me to "the first gospel," the word of God spoken in the immediate aftermath of our separation from

[3] *Further details can be found in the resource section, see page 154.*

him. His word was a promise. Though not fully understood for many generations, this word was *Jesus*. For God so loved the world that a plan had to be made; for God so loved the world that Jesus had to be sent. Though it broke the Father's heart, our disobedience was not a surprise to him. The plan was ready. No time was lost. The groundwork was laid the moment we fell.

Does this fill you with a sense of wonder? It should—for the protoevangelium is God saying to us, "I've loved you for longer than you can possibly imagine. I've been working to make a way home for you since before you were even born."

The story of Christmas begins farther back than we can really grasp—back before the darkness of our broken relationship with God. It begins with a love so unfathomable that everything concerning us, from our creation to our redemption, was undertaken in spite of all it would cost.

PRAYER & REFLECTION

* Read the following passage slowly and prayerfully:

  > At just the right time, when we were still powerless, Christ died for the ungodly. Very rarely will anyone die for a righteous person, though for a good person someone might possibly dare to die. But God demonstrates his own love for us in this: While we were still sinners, Christ died for us (ROMANS 5:6-8).

* The Apostle Paul's prayer for the Ephesians and for "all the Lord's holy people" was that they would be able to "grasp how wide and long and high and deep is the love of Christ, and to know this love that surpasses knowledge" (3:18-19). Take a few minutes to reflect upon the magnitude of God's love for *you*.

DECEMBER 1

Lamentation

Restore us, O God; make your face shine on us, that we may be saved. How long, Lord God Almighty, will your anger smoulder against the prayers of your people? You have fed them with the bread of tears; you have made them drink tears by the bowlful. You have made us an object of derision to our neighbours, and our enemies mock us. Restore us, God Almighty; make your face shine on us, that we may be saved.

PSALM 80:3-7

In recent decades, a new tradition has sprung up called "Blue Christmas." Have you heard of it? Hospitals, funeral homes and churches sometimes offer a seasonal service of worship that is especially designed for those who grieve at a time when all the world seems to be celebrating. Or that's how it started.

Very soon it became apparent that "those who grieve" are not the only group of people who feel alienated and alone during the month of December. Of those you know well, including yourself, how many have experienced a recent loss? How many are overwhelmed by fresh waves of grief, though their loss may have happened many years ago? How many are struggling financially? How many are distressed by family pressures, breakdowns, or conflicts? How many are lonely, suffering from illness, disappointed or hurting in some unnamed way—and made more aware of all this by the season? Is your list getting long? The truth is that we all experience challenges like these in varying degrees at different times in our lives. We all need space for "lamentation."

The Bible, and especially the Old Testament, is full of lamentation. Scripture doesn't "sugarcoat" the human experience, nor does God ask his people to "turn that frown upside-down." The psalms in particular set an example for us of how to bring every circumstance and emotion to the Father. The Bible's prayers of lament echo the cries of our own hearts in times of distress:

> "Out of the depths we cry to you, O Lord!"
>
> "We've known affliction, wandering, bitterness and gall, and our souls are downcast!"
>
> "You have fed us with the bread of tears! Restore us!"
>
> Our souls are overwhelmed with sorrow to the point of death... if it is possible, take this cup from us!"[4]

There is—or there should be—a place for lamentation in our corporate prayers.

The "Blue Christmas" service is a great idea. But I have a complaint to make of it. It implies that this one-day offering is for a small group of poor needy souls who just can't seem to get into the Christmas spirit. It is typically removed from regular programming so as to allow the rest of the community to carry on with the party. But this, too, is part of the problem.

In the beautiful rhythm of the Christian calendar, space is made for both "feasts" (times of celebration) and "fasts" (times of prayerful reflection and penance). There can be a tendency today to embrace the feasts—like Christmas and Easter—but to reject the fasts. Or, in the case of Advent, to

---

[4] *Paraphrased from Psalm 130:1; Lamentations 3:19-20; Psalm 80:5,7; and Matthew 26:38-39*

treat what was once a *penitential* season as a drawn-out celebration of Christmas—before Christmas actually arrives.

A faithful observance of Advent is one of quiet, sober reflection. It considers our darkness and our need. It lingers over psalms of lamentation. It remembers the long years of waiting for our salvation to appear. It examines God's promises and his faithfulness in keeping those promises. And it directs us to anticipate Christ's coming again, when our loving Father will wipe every tear from our eyes. In short, Advent is a season especially designed to resonate with those burdened by "blueness." It is even a season designed to call those of us who do *not* feel "blue" to slow down, to pause, and to remember why the promise of Christ's coming matters so much; and if we do not grieve ourselves, to take the time to "mourn" in solidarity with those who do (ROMANS 12:15).

As the world around us surges into a frenzied and festive December, let's take a step away from the party and ask the Holy Spirit to prepare our hearts for a deeper and truer celebration of Christmas—one that is not undermined by lamentation, but that is made more potent because of it.

PRAYER & REFLECTION

* Take a few minutes—without rushing—to do an "internal inventory." What burdens of "blueness" do you carry? How about those in your circle of close family and friends? Next, spend some time in prayer, offering these burdens and those who carry them to God's keeping. But don't finish there. Close your time by asking God to make you alert to the people in your life, church and community who struggle during Advent, and to teach you how to "mourn with those who mourn."

DECEMBER 2

Law, Sin, Death

No one will be declared righteous in God's sight by the works of the law; rather, through the law we become conscious of our sin.

ROMANS 3:20

In every human age, different imbalances are to be found. Sterner, past generations may have spoken too much about "fire and brimstone," but if we have a failing today, it is in speaking about God's love and mercy—without sparing a thought for the context which lends meaning to those attributes. That context is God's holiness.

In ancient times, God called a certain man to come out from his people, and to be distinct from them. This man, Abraham, was to be the father of a new nation. He and his descendants were chosen to live in a covenant relationship with God, and to carry with them the true story of human history. The world had forgotten the truth of where it came from, but through Abraham's family, God would reach out to those who were estranged from him by sin, and whose destiny was death.

Several generations passed. Abraham's descendants, the people of Israel, had become slaves in Egypt. God intervened. He led them out of that dark bondage. Then he gave them something extraordinary: his law. This was not just a set of rules. It was a revelation of his heart. Before the giving of the law, his people might have claimed ignorance. But the law revealed to us God's character: just, loving, morally perfect, faithful, compassionate... And those who were called *his people* were to *emulate him*:

> I am the Lord your God; consecrate yourselves and be holy, because I am holy (LEVITICUS 11:44).

God's people, then and now, are called to be like him. We are to honour him in everything. We are to love our neighbours as ourselves. Did we do it? Ever? No. We sinned. Our ancestors sinned; and we, personally and collectively, have sinned. And there is only one way in which God's holiness can respond to sin. The book of Isaiah explains it this way:

> Your iniquities have separated you from your God; your sins have hidden his face from you, so that he will not hear (59:2).

Scripture tells us that "the wages of sin is death" (ROMANS 6:23), and that "the wrath of God" is the natural consequence of human wickedness (ROMANS 1-2). So, the Bible makes it clear that our own actions, our own sin, separated us from our loving Creator, and resulted in our entirely deserved condemnation.

Is this too "theological," too "abstract," to accept? Consider with me a tale of human romance. One partner honours every part of his promises. His words and actions are irreproachable: good, kind, generous and faithful. The other partner's behaviour is "toxic." She willfully and repeatedly breaks every part of her commitment, inflicting continual heartbreak on a lover who has done nothing to deserve it. What would be a reasonable response on his part? Would he not be justified in walking away from this minefield? Should he not simply say, "She has made her choice. Let her live with the consequences of her actions," and "I'm better off without her"? Certainly he would be within his rights to do so, and few objective observers would find fault with him for it.

If the relationship between God and fallen humanity is a divine romance, this description is not far off. Though we might aspire to be just as flawless as our Lord, the law showed us that we are completely unable to live up to this standard. And we cannot of ourselves undo the consequences of that failure.

This is where unpleasant words like "sin," "death," and "wrath," give way to something more exhilarating than we could have imagined. Our divine lover *did not* choose to abandon us to the consequences of our actions. He sent his Son, to "fulfill all righteousness," and to offer "propitiation" for our sins—to do and pay all that we could neither do nor pay. It is only when we understand the outrage of our sin against a holy God, that we can begin to grasp the magnitude of a love willing to go so far for us.

PRAYER & REFLECTION

* What are your feelings when the subject of God's wrath is spoken of? Does it make you uncomfortable or insecure? If you are a Christian, then *know* that your sin has been paid for in full. You "have been made holy through the sacrifice of the body of Jesus Christ once for all" (HEBREWS 10:10). If you are not a Christian, then this confident standing before God is available to you also through the repentance of your sin and belief in Jesus Christ. The Bible tells us that God does not want *anyone* to "perish," but for all to come to him in repentance (2 PETER 3:9).
* Spend some time reflecting on God's holy character. Ask for his help in living a holy life.

DECEMBER 3

The Deliverer

The law is only a shadow of the good things that are coming—not the realities themselves.

HEBREWS 10:1

In the early days following Jesus' birth, his human parents were prompted to flee from the murderous intent of a jealous king named Herod. The little family took refuge in Egypt, a place rich with significance in the history of ancient Israel...

It was to Egypt that a young man named Joseph had been sold into slavery. Though betrayed by his brothers, he trusted in God, and obeyed him throughout his time of exile, in the end becoming a means of saving the very ones who had betrayed him (GENESIS 37-50). The holy infant who now took refuge in Egypt, would likewise know the betrayal of the very ones he came to save.

In Egypt, God's people were enslaved for generations. It was only through God's miraculous intervention that the people were able to flee to freedom. At the point of their escape, they celebrated the first passover, sacrificing an unblemished lamb and marking their homes with its blood so that they would be spared from a plague of death (EXODUS 12). The Christ-child who now took refuge in Egypt, had come to be the true passover Lamb.

In the years that followed their escape from Egypt, the Israelites wandered in the wilderness. They'd been given the law and they'd seen with their own eyes the power and kindness of their God. But when their road got hard, they sinned, speaking against God, and bringing upon themselves a plague of venomous serpents. They cried out to God for deliverance, and were saved from death if they would look to a bronze serpent set upon a pole (NUMBERS 21:4-9). This miraculous deliverance saved the people from sudden death in that moment, but it could not save them from their sins, nor from the death that would one day claim them.

After forty years in the wilderness, God's appointed leader led the Israelites into the good land he'd promised to them (JOSHUA 1-24). That leader's name was "Joshua," which means "God is deliverance." The Greek pronunciation of this Hebrew name is "Jesus"—the name given to the incarnate Son of God, who would one day lead his people to their eternal home.

In a sense, God's people are all exiles in this dark world, then and now, wherever they may be—for we are tempted and tried, we sin and we suffer. We cry out to God for deliverance.

Throughout the Old Testament, we meet heroes of faith who clung to God through their own failures and all the chaos and heartbreak that life in this world brings. We read their stories with awe, inspired by their examples, perhaps praying that God would move so powerfully in our day too. But scripture tells us this:

> These were all commended for their faith, yet none of them received what had been promised, since God had planned something better for us so that only together with us would they be made perfect (HEBREWS 11:39-40).

The author of Hebrews is speaking about Jesus. *We* have an advantage which all the heroes of ancient Israel did not have. We have seen more than mere shadows. We can read biblical history with the recognition that all of these things were pointing to one person, one answer, one hope for humanity.

The same passage in Hebrews continues with this word of exhortation:

> Since we are surrounded by such a great cloud of witnesses, let us throw off everything that hinders and the sin that so easily entangles. And let us run with perseverance the race marked out for us, fixing our eyes on Jesus... (12:1-2)

As the season of Advent progresses, let's fix our eyes on Jesus. Let's look *beyond* the comforting and familiar scenes of the nativity, and delve *so* deeply into all the richness of God's promise and all the wonders of Christ's person, that we forget the noise and distractions, and find joy and rest in the only Deliverer who can carry us through this life to "a better country" (HEBREWS 11:16).

PRAYER & REFLECTION

* The "collect" (prayer) for the fourth Sunday of Advent[5] speaks of our longing for the deliverance that only Jesus Christ can provide. Take some time to read slowly through the prayer—slowly enough to consider its words and add a few of your own:

  > Raise up, we beseech you, O Lord, your power, and come among us, and with great might succour us; that whereas, through our sins and wickedness, we are sore let and hindered in running the race that is set before us, your bountiful grace and mercy may speedily help and deliver us; who with the Father and the Holy Spirit lives and reigns, one God, world without end. Amen.

---

[5] *Further details can be found in the resource section, see pages 99 and 111.*

Week Two

WAITING ON THE WORD

The prophets searched intently and with the greatest care,
trying to find out the time and circumstances
to which the Spirit of Christ in them was pointing
when he predicted the sufferings of the Messiah
and the glories that would follow.

1 PETER 1:10-11

DECEMBER 4

Messengers

In the past God spoke to our ancestors through the prophets at many times and in various ways, but in these last days he has spoken to us by his Son.

HEBREWS 1:1-2

In Old Testament times, God appointed leaders of various kinds to guide and care for his people. These leaders included prophets, judges, priests, and kings.

Between God and his people, there was a barrier. Human sin had created a rift, and intermediaries were necessary. The judges and kings governed and led. The priests made sacrifices to God on behalf of the people. And the prophets were his messengers, tasked with speaking God's words to the people. The greatest of these messengers, according to Hebrew tradition, was Moses.

Moses' life had been a turbulent one—born into slavery, adopted into royalty, committing murder, and fleeing the country—all this we are told in a single chapter. Then, having settled and married in a land called Midian, Moses was tending his father-in-law's flock when God called to him from a burning bush. Moses' life was about to change.

Moses was not eager to take up the challenge that God set before him, and who could blame him? Confronting a powerful king who wanted him dead would only be the first step. Over the years, Moses would see God's power at work, and would speak to him "face to face" (EXODUS 33:11), but the people he led were often ornery and provoking.

When Moses came down from Mount Sinai, after receiving the law from God, the people "trembled with fear," and said to him:

> "Speak to us yourself and we will listen. But do not have God speak to us or we will die" (EXODUS 20:19).

The people knew their own sinful state and feared the power and holiness of God, but in spite of this they continued to disobey him. They persisted in disobedience across generations—in times of blessing and times of hardship—and the *messengers* of God were not received with respect.

Most of the prophets experienced persecution at the hands of those they were sent to serve, and many were killed by them. The hardening effect of sin produced open hostility towards both God's message and his messengers. The letter to the Hebrews summarises it this way:

> Some faced jeers and flogging, and even chains and imprisonment. They were put to death by stoning; they were sawed in two; they were killed by the sword... the world was not worthy of them (HEBREWS 11:36-38).

The Old Testament contains the records of many of these amazing saints. Though flawed human beings, they were given the privilege of delivering God's message. Often their messages pointed the people back to God's revealed will—the law—and called them to repent of their sin. Sometimes prophetic messages contained warnings and encouragements regarding future events. And always the role of the prophet brought with it the privilege of a unique relationship with both God and his people.

Could any position of privilege be less enviable? Were we to do an analysis of those who entered this "profession," which of us would wish it for ourselves—or for our children? Think about it. How many of the prophets were "happy"? Certainly not Jeremiah. How many lived in prosperity and security? Certainly not Elijah. How many had peaceful home lives? Certainly not Hosea. How many experienced "job satisfaction"? Certainly not Jonah.

To be a prophet was to speak hard words that people did not want to hear, and to receive in turn all the violence that they wanted to inflict upon God himself. Yet God, in his omniscience, surveyed all this, and decided to send one more messenger: his Son. We are given a striking illustration of this in one of Jesus' parables. It goes like this: over a period of time a landowner sent servants to visit his tenants and collect from them what was due...

> The tenants seized his servants; they beat one, killed another, and stoned a third. Then he sent other servants to them, more than the first time, and the tenants treated them the same way. Last of all, he sent his son to them. "They will respect my son," he said (MATTHEW 21:35-37).

Of course, they did *not* respect the son. They killed him also. And unlike the landowner in the parable, God knew in advance what the outcome would be.

There are three points that I want to draw attention to in all of this. Firstly, God's persistence in reaching out to a hostile people. Secondly, their—and our—unworthiness. And thirdly, the mind-blowing nature of God's sacrificial love for us in choosing to send his *Son* with his message.

PRAYER & REFLECTION

* Take some time to thank God for his persistence in reaching out to you. Are there ways in which you are unreceptive to his messages, especially when they carry a rebuke? Ask him to open your heart to hear and respond to his voice.

DECEMBER 5

The Divine Message

Jesus said, "For truly I tell you, many prophets and righteous people longed to see what you see but did not see it, and to hear what you hear but did not hear it."

MATTHEW 13:17

Two men were walking down a certain road headed out of Jerusalem. They were depressed. So much had happened in the last few years, and even more in the last few days. All their hopes had been swept up in these events, only to be dashed, like the snuffing out of a candle.

The road they walked along was headed to a village called Emmaus, and before their journey was complete, they met the risen Lord, though they did not at first recognise him. Jesus asked them to explain what had happened to discourage them so completely... and then, he opened their eyes. They'd heard the story, but they hadn't understood it. Luke's gospel tells it this way:

> Beginning with Moses and all the Prophets, he [Jesus] explained to them what was said in all the Scriptures concerning himself (LUKE 24:27).

What must this have been like? To hear the Word of God expounded and explained by the embodied Word of God?

Throughout human history, God has spoken. In various ways he has revealed to us what he is like, how we as his people should live, and how deeply he loves us. His message, recorded in the scriptures, is powerful and prophetic, "alive and active" (HEBREWS 4:12).

> For everything that was written in the past was written to teach us, so that through the endurance taught in the Scriptures and the encouragement they provide we might have hope (ROMANS 15:4).

When the writings in our New Testament speak of "the scriptures" they are referring to the divinely inspired words of the Hebrew scriptures, the *Old* Testament. This older revelation from God, however, was not complete. More was needed, and indeed, "more" had always been the plan. *Jesus* was that plan.

The New Testament tells us the story of Jesus, beginning with four gospel accounts of his earthly life, ministry, death and resurrection. Each account is slightly different in style and perspective, but John's gospel has a particularly unique voice, sometimes poetic, and always pointing to Jesus' divinity.

Who is Jesus? Each gospel writer must have pondered how to present the answer to readers in a coherent way. How do you begin to tell a story that's so filled with unfathomable truth? John's gospel begins by telling readers that Jesus is "the Word of God," in existence from the beginning, one with God, and integral to creation.

Later in the gospel narratives we find awe-inspiring accounts of the knowledge and power of this incarnate Word: the child Jesus instructing the teachers in the temple; crowds amazed by his teaching; storms, spirits and sickness all obedient to his command. *Who exactly* IS *this Jesus?* He's the embodied message of God to us—a message of reconciliation, love and hope.

You and I did not walk by his side on the road to Emmaus. We did not hear his voice or look into his eyes. But all the benefit of this divine revelation is ours in the written record of the New Testament. We inhabit a privileged moment in time. Not only do we have the Old Testament record of the promise and the example of its saints, but we have the record of those promises fulfilled in Jesus Christ, and the indwelling Holy Spirit to illuminate our understanding.

If you could walk for one hour along that road to Emmaus by the side of the resurrected Word of God, would you shrug it off? If you had in your home a written record of God's own message of love to you, would you take it for granted? Very likely you've been presented with these questions before, but they are worth revisiting and revisiting again. It's easy for us to forget what a gift we've been given in the scriptures, and to lose our sense of awe at the wonderful message contained therein. The road to Emmaus awaits. What will you do about it?

PRAYER & REFLECTION

* Have you neglected spending time with the Word? *(Books like this one are great tools, but they are no substitute for time spent in the Bible!)* Seek God's help in starting afresh.
* The "collect" (prayer) for the second Sunday of Advent[1] focuses on the gift of the Bible. Read it through, considering its words and adding a few of your own:

> Blessed Lord, who has caused all holy scriptures to be written for our learning: Grant that we may in such a way hear them, read, mark, learn, and inwardly digest them, that by patience and comfort of your holy Word, we may embrace and ever hold fast the blessed hope of everlasting life, which you have given us in our Saviour Jesus Christ. Amen.

[1] *Further details can be found in the resource section, see pages 99 and 105.*

DECEMBER 6

Cries of Longing

Drop down, ye heavens, from above,
and let the skies pour down righteousness.

ISAIAH 45:8a (KJV)

One of the things I love most about liturgical worship is the way it helps me to express the longings of my own heart through the words of scripture—especially during those times when it can be a struggle to put my thoughts and feelings into words.

In the ancient worship of Israel, psalms and other sacred texts were sung or chanted. This was done in various styles and settings, but always in a way that drew worshippers to *participate* in the prayers, praises, lamentations and longings of the scriptures. The earliest Christian liturgies took inspiration from temple worship, but layered and expanded upon it according to the new revelation they'd received in Jesus Christ.

One of the ancient chants of the Church, used for centuries during the season of Advent, is called "Rorate Cæli,"[2] Latin for "Drop down, ye heavens." This text from Isaiah forms a repeating refrain, a responsive supplication, throughout the chant: *"Drop down, ye heavens, from above, and let the skies pour down righteousness."*

The verses of the chant are also woven from the words of the Old Testament prophets, and describe an experience of darkness that we can still relate to today: sin, oppres-

[2] *The full text of Rorate Cæli is included in the resource section,* *see page 121.*

sion, lives and communities in chaos. The plea of faithful hearts, then and now, is for God to save his people in accordance with his promises.

Drop down, ye heavens! The prophet's poetic phrasing stirs the spirit. What better way is there to articulate the yearning of generations—that God might intervene, saving us from all that we need saving from? What better way to speak of Jesus' incarnation, his coming among us, than with this image of heaven coming down from above?

The traditional worship of Advent, and especially Rorate Cæli, urges us to join our prayers with the prayers of the saints who went before us. It invites us to express our longing for God's justice and mercy to break into our fallen world.

Scripture tell us that all of creation has been longing for God's redemption, a redemption bought by Jesus at his death, but still to be fully realised:

> We know that the whole creation has been groaning as in the pains of childbirth right up to the present time. Not only so, but we ourselves, who have the firstfruits of the Spirit, groan inwardly as we wait eagerly for our adoption to sonship, the redemption of our bodies (ROMANS 8:22-23).

In the same way that the Old Testament prophets and psalmists cried out to the Lord, we also cry out. When we pray with the words of scripture, we are not just remembering something that had meaning for the saints in ancient times, but we are entering into supplications that are just as relevant to our lives now. Moreover, when we cry out to God and "groan inwardly" it is not an expression of despair, but a statement of faith—because in doing so, we are gathering up all that we experience, and addressing it to the one who cares and is able to make things right.

Even during the joyful seasons of our lives, this world can never fully satisfy us. In fact, this world *shouldn't* fully satisfy us. Because we were made for more. We were made to be in perfect communion with our Creator. The Psalms provide us with this insight:

> "In thy presence is fullness of joy; at thy right hand there are pleasures for evermore" (PSALM 16:11 KJV).

To long in this way for the joy of heaven, the bliss of being together with our Lord, is both natural and right. Moreover, it is a longing which we know will one day be fulfilled. And so it makes sense that Rorate Cæli closes with a confident word about God's promise:

> Comfort ye, comfort ye my people;
> my salvation shall not tarry...
> Fear not, for I will save thee:
> For I am the Lord thy God,
> the Holy One of Israel, thy Redeemer.

PRAYER & REFLECTION

* Turn to the resource section and prayerfully read through Rorate Cæli (page 121). Alternatively, write your own verses, giving voice, in your own words, to your longings. Pause after each petition to repeat one of these verses:

  > I call on you, my God, for you will answer me; turn your ear to me and hear my prayer (PSALM 17:6).
  >
  > But as for me, I watch in hope for the Lord, I wait for God my Saviour; my God will hear me (MICAH 7:7).
  >
  > This is what the Lord says: "In the time of my favour I will answer you, and in the day of salvation I will help you" (ISAIAH 49:8).

DECEMBER 7

Justice & Mercy

Mercy and truth are met together;
righteousness and peace have kissed each other.

PSALM 85:10 (KJV)

During the early Church period, one of the most troublesome heresies that cropped up was Marcionism. Marcion, its founder, did not believe that the God of the Old Testament was the same being as the Father of Jesus Christ we read about in the New Testament. Though most Christians today would recognise this to be false, we can sometimes be misled in a similar way in thinking that the *character* of God is inconsistent—righteous and just in the Old Testament versus loving and merciful in the New. It's important for us to know that this is not the message revealed in scripture.

Proponents of a modern Marcion-esque view are apt to forget the less popular words and acts of Jesus. He told multiple parables which ended with the wicked being thrown into a place of darkness, weeping, and gnashing teeth (MATTHEW 8:12, 22:13, 25:30). With violent force he drove merchants out of the temple, over-turning tables and brandishing a whip (JOHN 2:13-16). He said, "I did not come to bring peace, but a sword" (MATTHEW 10:34).

Jesus was—and is—God the Son, "the same yesterday and today and forever" (HEBREWS 13:8). Throughout his earthly ministry he demonstrated that he had not come to "abolish" the Old Testament "law and prophets," but rather to "fulfill" them (MATTHEW 5:17). The law was not the invention of an over-zealous draconian schoolmaster. Jesus understood this. He was intimately familiar, not only with the technicalities of the law ("the letter"), but with its spirit.

When we earnestly examine the law, what can we expect to find? A harsh set of commandments? No. If we look closely, we will discover what the psalmists did—that they reveal a God in whom justice and mercy meet. In the law we find rules and principles which, if followed, will lead to human flourishing. In it we find a concern for the most disadvantaged members of society. In it we find a system which codifies second chances—we find the roots of redemption.

We need to pause to examine this word, *redemption*. In the context of the law, it referred to a payment being made to clear a debt, to regain someone's freedom or buy back an inheritance. It required action by someone with the right and the means necessary to intervene. The redemption laws were established to provide hope to those who might otherwise become impoverished and destitute for generations. In God's economy, such harms could be undone. Good could be made to come out of something that was not good.

In the biblical love story of Ruth we find an example of this at work. Ruth was a refugee widow, who moved to the land of Canaan with her mother-in-law Naomi, where they lived in poverty. Though the story begins in tragedy, it ends in joy. In exactly the way that the redemption laws intended, a wealthy kinsman named Boaz stepped in and married Ruth, taking it upon himself to raise an heir in the name of her first husband, thus providing grandchildren for Naomi and security for both women. It's a strange tale to modern ears, but it tells us a great deal about the character of God, as well as the heart—the spirit—of the Old Testament law.

God sees those who humans routinely overlook. He hears the cries of the destitute. And he cares. His law teaches his people to show kindness and fairness towards the disadvantaged. The psalms are filled with assurances that God hears when we call to him in distress. Now, this is not a guarantee that he will always work in our lives in the way we want him to. It does, however, point us to his response to our *deepest* need.

God knew that we were utterly unable to free ourselves from sin and darkness. *We* needed redemption: someone with the right and the means to intervene on our behalf; someone who could pay a price that we could not; someone who could bring good out of bad.

We cannot separate the just and merciful God who created the very concept of redemption from the Father who sent Jesus to be our Redeemer. In Jesus, the God who has always been compassionate towards the needy has provided for our greatest need: our debt paid, our freedom gained, and our heavenly inheritance secured.

PRAYER & REFLECTION

* When you think about the character of God, which aspects do you gravitate towards? If you gravitate towards his holiness, righteousness and justice, spend some time reflecting on his compassion and love. Or vice versa.

* In the midst of great calamity, a man named Job found faith to pray these words:

  > "I know that my redeemer lives, and that in the end he will stand on the earth" (JOB 19:25).

  Spend some time with these words, reflecting on the hope we have in our great Redeemer Jesus Christ.

DECEMBER 8

Tabernacle

"I will consecrate the tent of meeting and the altar and will consecrate Aaron and his sons to serve me as priests. Then I will dwell among the Israelites and be their God."

EXODUS 29:44-45

The book of Exodus tells the action-packed story of Israel escaping bondage in Egypt. It opens with signs and plagues, murder and miracles. Then, for the space of six chapters, the action is put on hold while meticulous details are given for the construction of a tabernacle and the costuming of its priests. It feels anticlimactic. Why should this minutiae have been given such prominence in the text? Why did it matter?

The tabernacle was God's "dwelling-place"[3] with his people. It was to be crafted using the best materials and the best skills available; by this it would be shown that the place where God resided was both sacred and royal. Moreover, these details were rich with meaning—and with foreshadowing.

In the most sacred part of the tabernacle, the holiest of things were kept: the ark, the bread of the presence, and the lampstand. In this we find a picture of God, and of his loving work on our behalf: the forgiveness of the Father in the mercy seat of the ark, the sacrifice of the Son in the memorial bread, and the illumination of the Holy Spirit in the lit menorah.

---

[3] *The word "tabernacle" literally means "dwelling-place."*

Over many centuries, the people of Israel were the keepers of these holy mysteries, though access was always restricted. This holiest of places in the tabernacle was separated from the outer area by a veil:

> But only the high priest entered the inner room, and that only once a year, and never without blood, which he offered for himself and for the sins the people had committed in ignorance (HEBREWS 9:7).

In the old covenant, priests were needed to represent human beings to God. The estrangement caused by sin could only be undone by sacrifice, and the sacrificial system was elaborate. But note this: the system of priests, sacrifices, and ceremonies was never intended to be the final solution. It was intended to point the way to the one person who would *be* the final solution.

We needed a greater *priest*, one whose sinlessness would enable him to enter God's presence unimpeded. We needed a priest who would live forever to intercede on our behalf, whose work could not be ended by death.

We needed a perfect *sacrifice*, one that did not have to be repeated year in and year out, one that would be effective and everlasting. The "blood of bulls and goats" was just a "shadow." We needed the real thing (HEBREWS 10).

We needed a better way for God to dwell with us, to "*tabernacle*" with us. We needed to be closer to our Lord—not to be kept at arm's length by physical barriers and ceremonial formality, but to know that he is immanent, present with us always, intimately and personally so.

The answer was Jesus. Jesus was to be our great high priest. Jesus was to be the final sacrifice. Jesus was to become incarnate, take on flesh, and dwell among us.

It was all foreshadowed in Exodus. Though many would refuse to accept it, the tabernacle and its ceremonies were merely temporary precursors. Yet, even to say this, fails to capture the whole picture. The Bible tells us that Jesus Christ, our great high priest,

> did not enter a sanctuary made with human hands that was only a copy of the true one; he entered heaven itself, now to appear for us in God's presence (HEBREWS 9:24).

Did you catch that? The old system and the tabernacle itself didn't come *first* at all. They were *copies*. They were meant to echo a reality outside of earthly time and space. Heaven was always the destination, and Jesus was always the way. And one day we will dwell with him there:

> "Look! God's dwelling place is now among the people, and he will dwell with them. They will be his people, and God himself will be with them and be their God" (REVELATION 21:3).

PRAYER & REFLECTION

* Spend some time reflecting upon Jesus' priestly work on your behalf and all that he has accomplished for you. Use the following passage to focus your thoughts and prayers:

> Therefore, since we have a great high priest who has ascended into heaven, Jesus the Son of God, let us hold firmly to the faith we profess. For we do not have a high priest who is unable to empathise with our weaknesses, but we have one who has been tempted in every way, just as we are—yet he did not sin. Let us then approach God's throne of grace with confidence, so that we may receive mercy and find grace to help us in our time of need (HEBREWS 4:14-16).

DECEMBER 9

The True King

Samuel told all the words of the Lord to the people who were asking him for a king. He said, "This is what the king who will reign over you will claim as his rights: He will take your sons and make them serve... He will take your daughters... He will take the best of your fields and vineyards and olive groves and give them to his attendants..."

But the people refused to listen to Samuel. "No!" they said. "We want a king over us. Then we will be like all the other nations."

1 SAMUEL 8:10-20

The people of Israel were *not* like other nations. They'd been chosen by God. He'd delivered them from slavery. When they were hungry in the wilderness, he fed them with "the bread of heaven" (EXODUS 16:4). He gave them the law, and took them to the good land of Canaan. He'd provided them with leaders: prophets, priests and judges, to govern, guide and intercede for them. And he, himself—God—was their king.

Like short-sighted children, the Israelites looked at all that God had given to them, and instead of being filled with awe and gratitude, they rejected it. They wanted to be "like all the other nations." That is, they wanted to be more like the very people that God had called them out from. They wanted to go backwards.

They were warned. Each and every human king that could be found to lead would be flawed. The power of such a position would, in one way or another, cause each one to abuse that position for selfish ends. And over the centuries, this is exactly what happened. There were comparatively good kings and there were spectacularly bad kings; but even the good kings abused their power. Eventually the kingdom fell. First, it was split in two, and then each half was conquered by an enemy empire. That's the summary. But we can't sum up the history of the kings of ancient Israel without taking a moment to talk about David.

David is the Old Testament archetype of a *good* human king. For some of us this rankles because we remember that David was a womanizer, an adulterer, and a murderer. We remember the moments in which his resolve was weak or his purposes selfish. We remember all the ways in which he fulfilled that original warning about human kings. There was, however, something more to David's reign, something which raised him above his sins and failures to be called "a man after God's own heart" (1 SAMUEL 13:14, ACTS 13:22). David was a shepherd who risked his life to protect his flock. David was a ruler willing to repent when confronted with the evil he'd done. David was a contemplative who loved to think about God's character and his law. During David's reign, the kingdom of Israel prospered. Though he did not always measure up, David desired and sought to honour God in all he did. In terms of human leadership, David was as good as it got, for all of these reasons.

It took God's people a very long time to learn the truth of what he'd told them back at the beginning. They had exchanged the very thing they needed for something that could never promote their wellbeing. They had exchanged their true king for a flawed shadow-version.

They needed something more than a human king. They needed an "anointed one," a "Messiah," who was able to do and be all that David was at his best—but one who was able to honour God wholly, to establish and eternally reign over a kingdom the likes of which had never been known. Such a king, God promised to one day provide:

> The government will be on his shoulders. And he will be called Wonderful Counsellor, Mighty God, Everlasting Father, Prince of Peace. Of the greatness of his government and peace there will be no end. He will reign on David's throne and over his kingdom, establishing and upholding it with justice and righteousness from that time on and forever (ISAIAH 9:6-7).

Jesus came to be this king. He was born into humility. He witnessed the tyranny of powerful men and understood the loving care of good shepherds. He lamented Israel's rejection of their true king. He was sent to his own people, though they did not recognise him. He would lay down his life to save them. And one day this king will return in glory and power, riding on the clouds, shining like the sun, and the angels will sing:

> Worthy is the Lamb, who was slain, to receive power and wealth and wisdom and strength and honour and glory and praise (REVELATION 5:12)!

PRAYER & REFLECTION

* Spend some time reflecting upon the festive events of the first Palm Sunday (SEE JOHN 12:12-16). On that day, Jesus entered Jerusalem, where he would soon be killed, and the crowds greeted him with praises that spoke truth beyond their understanding:

> *"Hosanna! Blessed is he who comes in the name of the Lord! Blessed is the* king *of Israel!"*

DECEMBER 10

Faithfulness in Waiting

All these people were still living by faith when they died. They did not receive the things promised; they only saw them and welcomed them from a distance, admitting that they were foreigners and strangers on earth.

HEBREWS 11:13

We live in an age of instant results. Text messages and video calls can immediately connect us with friends on the other side of the planet. Random curiosities can be satisfied in a nanosecond with a simple search query. The idea of waiting for anything goes against the grain of our culture, and more and more we find that we lack the attention span required to maintain interest in anything that cannot be had as soon as it is wanted.

Hebrews 11 is a magnificent and inspiring passage. It summarises the feats of many saints of the Old Testament period, and reminds us that *the whole* of their lives were spent waiting—and waiting for something that did not come in their lifetimes: the Messiah. We look to their examples because they were faithful, and their faithfulness was marked by patient, hopeful, obedient waiting. Though their immediate circumstances were often difficult, these men and women placed their confidence in God's promises. They were looking forward to "a better resurrection." In a similar way, the epistle to the Hebrews goes on to challenge New Testament believers to "fix our eyes on Jesus" so that we might not "grow weary and lose heart" (HEBREWS 12:2-3). In the midst of all the distractions of modern life, an eternal perspective can do for us what it did for the saints who went before us.

When Mary and Joseph brought the infant Jesus to the temple, they were greeted by two more examples of enduring faith: Simeon and Anna. Both were old; they had lived for many years in a disheartening period of Israel's history. And yet both rejoiced, simply to be able to see with their own eyes this new chapter of God's promise unfolding.

How do we fare by comparison to these saints? Are our lives characterised by patient, hopeful obedience? Or do we seek to distract ourselves from a seemingly endless vigil? Do we trust that God will do all that he has promised? Have we surrendered to him the need to control the details of our lives? Have we learned to say, with our Saviour, "not my will, but thine be done" (LUKE 22:42 KJV)? These are not easy questions. Faithfulness in waiting may *sound* simple, but it is hard work.

Advent offers us an opportunity to put this discipline into practice by waiting until Christmas to celebrate the incarnation of our Lord. The centuries-old tradition of the crèche is one small way that households (and churches) can mark the Advent journey with a spirit of patient waiting. Though the terms "crèche" and "nativity display" are often used interchangeably, we should make a distinction. The crèche tradition does not involve erecting a full nativity scene in early December and leaving it up for four weeks! Such displays are certainly welcome reminders that Jesus is central to our seasonal celebrations, but they fall short because they fail to help us heed the Advent message of waiting. The crèche tradition is designed to be a slow-moving re-enactment. The inn's stable is set up during the season of Advent, *but stands empty*. Figurines depicting Mary and Joseph begin the season across a mantelpiece or in another part of the room, making their journey slowly, day by day, until they reach the stable on Christmas Eve. The baby Jesus does not appear until Christmas. And the magi do not make their appearance until Epiphany (twelve days later on January 6). This simple, family-friendly tradition has the power to remind us of the patient, hopeful obedience which was so indispensable to the saints who went before us, our ancestors in the faith.

Like the believers of the Old Testament, we, too, are called to faithfulness in waiting. Though we have privileges they did not, we still live in a broken and often disheartening world. Though we remember with gratitude and awe all that Jesus did at his first coming, we are still awaiting his second coming. Our lives are imperfect. We struggle to remain focused on God's plan and on his priorities. We struggle to surrender to his timing. Observing a true Advent can help—to lengthen our attention spans, to reset our expectations, and to teach us patience.

PRAYER & REFLECTION

* In what ways do you feel yourself to be in a place of waiting in life? What is it that you are waiting for? Are you longing for eternity with your Lord, or for something you hope will make a paradise of your earthly life? Is your waiting characterised by a resentful spirit or patient trust? Offer your desires to God, asking for his wisdom, and his help in waiting.
* Spend some time meditating on the song of Simeon, making note of his posture and priorities:

  > Sovereign Lord, as you have promised, you may now dismiss your servant in peace. For my eyes have seen your salvation, which you have prepared in the sight of all nations: a light for revelation to the Gentiles, and the glory of your people Israel (LUKE 2:29-32).

Week Three

PREPARING THE WAY

"Prepare the way for the Lord,
make straight paths for him."

MATTHEW 3:3

DECEMBER 11

The Lord Remembers

In the time of Herod king of Judea there was a priest named Zechariah, who belonged to the priestly division of Abijah; his wife Elizabeth was also a descendant of Aaron. Both of them were righteous in the sight of God, observing all the Lord's commands and decrees blamelessly. But they were childless because Elizabeth was not able to conceive, and they were both very old.

LUKE 1:5-7

It had been four hundred years since a prophet had last been sent to the people of Israel—that's a *very* long dry spell. And these centuries had been marked by oppression and revolt, culminating in the conquest of Jerusalem and its surrounding areas by the Roman Empire in 63 BC. A brutal and decadent puppet king by the name of Herod had been set up over the region. The situation was discouraging, almost to the point of hopelessness.

There are elements of that time that we may relate to—ruthlessness and corruption amongst the powerful, rampant immorality saturating the culture, restlessness and despair fuelling violent protests. These were godless times. But even in so-called godless times, godly people can still be found, and God is still at work.

Zechariah and Elizabeth were godly people. Elderly and barren, this couple had given up hoping that God might bless them with a child. It was no longer possible. There had been no point continuing with their prayers on the subject for many years now. But God had a plan to break into this hopeless moment in time—and they were to be a part of it.

Zechariah's name, a common one in that day, means "the Lord remembers," and this man's place in the gospel story shows us that God did not forget his people, nor this faithful couple. Like many believers today, they had offered their cherished hopes to their heavenly Father, and accepted that his "No" was spoken in love. It is evident that they believed God's answer was "No," because of Zechariah's reaction when an angel suddenly appeared and informed him that those long-shelved prayers were about to be answered... *with a "Yes."* His reaction was astonishment and incredulity. He and Elizabeth were to welcome a son. The child was to be called *John,* a name which means "the Lord is gracious," and this child was a sign of God's grace—to a childless couple, to the people of that day, and to every generation since. This child was to be the first prophet in four centuries, with an utterly unique role to play. The angel explained:

> "He will be filled with the Holy Spirit even before he is born. He will bring back many of the people of Israel to the Lord their God. And he will go on before the Lord, in the spirit and power of Elijah, to turn the hearts of the parents to their children and the disobedient to the wisdom of the righteous—to make ready a people prepared for the Lord" (LUKE 1:15-17).

Chances are you know how the story of John's birth unfolded. Zechariah was struck dumb for his disbelief, and his power of speech only returned when his son, John the Baptist, was born and named. When Zechariah was again able to speak, his first words were of praise to God for how he'd remembered his promises, and was even now preparing the way of salvation for his people.

PRAYER & REFLECTION

* Can you relate to a period of time in which God seemed silent and aloof? Be encouraged. He is present and working, even when we cannot see how. Bring before the Lord the concerns you have for your own life and the world at large, remembering especially those things you may have given up on praying for.
* Set aside some time to read through Zechariah's prophetic song of praise (below). Note how these verses point to a God who sees the true needs of his people, and cares for them.

> Praise be to the Lord, the God of Israel, because he has come to his people and redeemed them.
>
> He has raised up a horn of salvation for us in the house of his servant David (as he said through his holy prophets of long ago), salvation from our enemies and from the hand of all who hate us—to show mercy to our ancestors and to remember his holy covenant, the oath he swore to our father Abraham: to rescue us from the hand of our enemies, and to enable us to serve him without fear in holiness and righteousness before him all our days.
>
> And you, my child, will be called a prophet of the Most High; for you will go on before the Lord to prepare the way for him, to give his people the knowledge of salvation through the forgiveness of their sins, because of the tender mercy of our God, by which the rising sun will come to us from heaven to shine on those living in darkness and in the shadow of death, to guide our feet into the path of peace (LUKE 1:68-79).

DECEMBER 12

Forerunner

In those days John the Baptist came, preaching in the wilderness of Judea and saying, "Repent, for the kingdom of heaven has come near." This is he who was spoken of through the prophet Isaiah:

"A voice of one calling in the wilderness,
'Prepare the way for the Lord,
make straight paths for him.'"

MATTHEW 3:1-3

The ancient Christian calendar strikes a rhythm between feast and fast, that is, between seasons of celebration and seasons of penitence. There is a timeless wisdom in this rhythm—because the human experience is not static. During the course of a single Christian life there will be both rejoicing and weeping, cause for thanksgiving and for repentance. The ancient calendar makes room for it all, and calls us to orient our hearts towards God on every occasion.

We live in an age that shuns the idea of fasting and penitence. As a culture, we're quick to embrace the celebratory festivals of Easter and Christmas, but often we're equally quick to dismiss the idea that these festivals require sober preparation. Advent, like Lent, is meant to be just such a season.

Perhaps this seems strange to us today, though if we think about the events that led up to that first Christmas, sober preparation makes sense. A "forerunner" was appointed at Jesus' first coming. John the Baptist was the last of the prophets belonging to the Old Testament line, and it was his job to prepare God's people for the coming of the Messiah. This preparation time—and its ambassador—were very far from being light-hearted or celebratory:

> John's clothes were made of camel's hair, and he had a leather belt around his waist. His food was locusts and wild honey. People went out to him from Jerusalem and all Judea and the whole region of the Jordan. Confessing their sins, they were baptised by him in the Jordan River (MATTHEW 3:4-6).

The hearts of God's people were to be prepared for the start of Jesus' earthly ministry *through repentance*. They listened to John's somber preaching, they confessed their sins, and they underwent ceremonial cleansing. Penitence is what prepared them for a new chapter.

The season of Advent is not only a new chapter; it is the Christian New Year, and draws its inspiration from the Jewish New Year (as it was observed at the time of the early Church). The Jewish New Year included two "high holy days" and a period of ten days in between which were marked by fasting, prayer and repentance. The themes of this season included the creation (and fall) of humanity, the coming day of judgement, and an appeal to God for atonement. Those same themes are echoed in Advent. We remember our need to repent, the coming day of judgement, and the promises and prophesies of a Saviour.

Though Advent is undeniably a season of penitence, it is also a season of hope—because there *is* a Saviour who *has* made atonement for us, and we have confidence that:

> If we confess our sins, God is faithful and just and will forgive us our sins and purify us from all unrighteousness (1 JOHN 1:9).

Moreover, because of this, we do not fear the second coming (*"adventus"* in Latin) of our Lord Jesus, even though he will return not as a humble baby, but in power and glory as king and judge.

Scripture is filled with exhortations to believers of how to live during these "last days" as we await the return of our Lord Jesus Christ. We are to be prayerful, alert, "of sober mind" (1 PETER 4:7). We are to preach sound doctrine, even when it is unwelcome (2 TIMOTHY 4:1-5). We are to live holy, quiet lives, encouraging one another with the promise of heaven (1 THESSALONIANS 4).

The season of Advent takes its tone from these scriptural exhortations regarding the last days, and from the example of John the Baptist. It calls us to step away from the frivolity that so often occupies our attention at this time of year, to quiet our hearts and minds, and think deeply and seriously about what it means to live in prayerful expectation of the *adventus* of our Lord.

PRAYER & REFLECTION

* The "collect" (prayer) for the third Sunday of Advent[1] focuses on our need to prepare our hearts for both "comings" of Jesus. Take some time to read slowly through the prayer—slowly enough to consider its words and add a few of your own:

  > O Lord Jesus Christ, who at your first coming sent your messenger to prepare the way before you: Grant that the ministers and stewards of your mysteries may likewise so prepare and make ready your way, by turning the hearts of the disobedient to the wisdom of the just, that at your second coming to judge the world we may be found an acceptable people in your sight; who lives and reigns with the Father and the Holy Spirit, ever one God, world without end. Amen.

---

[1] *Further details can be found in the resource section, see pages 99 and 108.*

DECEMBER 13

Metanoia

"Even now," declares the Lord, "return to me with all your heart, with fasting and weeping and mourning."

Rend your heart and not your garments.

JOEL 2:12-13

Hypocrisy is a part of the human condition. It always has been. It's born out of pride and deception, and it is how every one of us is tempted to behave when we want others to believe that we are something other than what we *really* are. Sometimes we can fool strangers or even those close to us. We can speak the right words, wear the right clothes, adopt the right postures—and be believed. But God does not want our hypocrisy. And he can see through it.

For centuries, the people of Israel had the benefit of the law and the prophets. They knew what sin was. And they knew the words and rituals required to be considered righteous. Again and again, the prophets had to tell them to humble themselves, to confess, to return—and not just with words and meaningless gestures, but with their lives.

True repentance isn't casual or half-hearted. It involves an honest acknowledgment of what we've done, sincere contrition, and a course correction, that is, turning back to God.

Hypocrisy is destructive. Not only does it make a mockery of God's grace, but it can devastate those who have looked up to our example of faith. This is true whether we are leaders of an international parachurch organisation or whether we teach Sunday school in a local congregation; whether we are grandparents to a dozen young people, or whether we've been a believing friend to one lost soul.

The habit of hypocrisy is the reason John the Baptist had such harsh words for the Pharisees. It was not because they were serious-minded and pious, genuinely caring about holiness. No, these faith leaders only *claimed* to be virtuous, but they used their positions of power to oppress others. They were perfectly willing to go through the right ceremonies, speak the right words, and then carry on with business as usual. But John's words to them were that they must "produce *fruit* in keeping with repentance" (MATTHEW 3:8).

The ceremonies were not enough. The right words were not enough. The call to repentance was a call to *metanoia*. That's the Greek word used in the New Testament, and it means transformation or conversion—a change of heart and mind that results in a changed life. And such a transformed way of living is only possible when we invite our Lord into everything we do and are.

*

There is an ancient prayer of penitence and intercession that dates back to the fourth century. It's simply called "the Litany,"[2] and it appeals to God for his forgiveness and aid in every aspect of life. A few generations ago, it was not uncommon for the Litany to be used on a weekly basis, but no longer. The Litany's penitential nature has made it unfashionable, though it is as relevant as ever. Some traditional churches and religious communities still make it their practice to begin the season of Advent by walking

---

[2] *Further details can be found on page 114 of the resource section.*

prayerfully through their place of worship, saying or singing words that include these petitions:

> Remember not, Lord, our offences, nor the offences of our forefathers...
>
> From pride, vainglory, and hypocrisy, good Lord, deliver us...
>
> To give us true repentance... and to endue us with the grace of your Holy Spirit to amend our lives according to your holy Word, we beseech you, good Lord.

The Litany acknowledges the need for God's forgiveness and redemptive work to touch every aspect of our lives, and this includes our personal lives and our churches, our neighbourhoods, industries and governments. As is true with every prayer—including spontaneous ones—the Litany's value is in our willingness to enter into the meaning of the words, to speak them from our hearts.

Though penitence is never "fun," it is rooted in hope and has the power to produce genuine joy. Penitence was never meant to trap us in a place of shame and condemnation; rather, it is a gateway from despair to freedom. We enter into the liberation of repentance knowing that Jesus came for the express purpose of saving sinners like us (1 TIMOTHY 1:15), knowing that if we will repent, we are assured of his forgiveness (1 JOHN 1:9), and knowing that our repentance produces rejoicing in heaven (LUKE 15:7,10).

PRAYER & REFLECTION

* Spend some time in prayer. Begin by asking God to give you "true repentance." Next, make your confession to the Lord. You may wish to use your own words, or the words of the Litany (see page 114).

DECEMBER 14

Becoming Less

"I am the Lord's servant," Mary answered.
"May your word to me be fulfilled."

LUKE 1:38

Those of us who love the scriptures often seek to use our imaginations to "fill in the details." Imagination is, after all, a gift. We may write fictional accounts or act out dramatic interpretations of biblical narratives. These can help to engage us in the story or to reflect upon key features of the text—but they can also distract and distort. In our fallen world, even with the best of intentions, human imagination does not always produce helpful results.

Where Mary is concerned, people of faith have often wished to know more than what scripture reveals. It is certainly true that she had a unique role to play. Held in highest honour by early Christians, later generations went further, giving Mary such titles as "Queen of heaven" and "God-bearer," and commissioning famous artists to depict her presiding in palaces swathed in luxurious robes. What arguably began as imaginative ways to pay tribute to a great woman of faith, later became embedded in dogma, a distraction and a distortion of the message of scripture.

Believers today have the task of pulling back layers from centuries of embellishment and enactments, and doing our best to simply see what the gospel writers intended us to see.

Of all the gospel writers, it is Luke who gives us the most detailed portrait of Mary. She was a virgin of Nazareth and betrothed, when an angel appeared to her and addressed her as "highly favoured." This address was not made to a queen in a palace, but to a modest young woman destined to be a carpenter's wife. Being addressed in this way troubled her. She did not understand it...

> But the angel said to her, "Do not be afraid, Mary; you have found favour with God. You will conceive and give birth to a son, and you are to call him Jesus. He will be great and will be called the Son of the Most High. The Lord God will give him the throne of his father David, and he will reign over Jacob's descendants forever; his kingdom will never end."
>
> "How will this be," Mary asked the angel, "since I am a virgin?"
>
> The angel answered, "The Holy Spirit will come on you, and the power of the Most High will overshadow you. So the holy one to be born will be called the Son of God..."
>
> "I am the Lord's servant," Mary answered. "May your word to me be fulfilled" (LUKE 1:30-38).

Throughout the interview with the angel we find Mary's defining characteristics to be humble honesty and holy obedience. When the angel told her what was to happen, she did not posture. She just admitted that she didn't understand the logistics. And when the angel finished explaining, she spoke a word of simple acquiescence. Though she understood from the angel's information that she was being given a unique place of honour beyond all imagination, we never read of Mary putting on airs.

It was John the Baptist who said about Jesus, "He must become greater, I must become less" (JOHN 3:30), but Mary would have resonated with these words. Like John the Baptist, she understood that all this was not really about her, but about Jesus. Mary's son would be great, a king, reigning forever. But God did not choose a princess to bear this child. He chose a humble woman of virtue. Here was a woman who was not putting herself forward, not seeking opportunities to push into the spotlight, but was simply willing to do and be whatever God asked of her. And her humble trust bore the fruit of obedience.

Where Mary is concerned we can sometimes fall into the opposite error of the medieval Church. Determined not to venerate Mary too much, we can avoid her altogether. But Mary *was* a shining example to saints of every age. And notice this—she was not the sort of "modern" heroine that we tend to admire today. She was not commended as an entrepreneur or an activist, a great writer or leader, a parvenu or a networker. She was celebrated simply for being a humble and obedient believer in God. And when blessed, she gave him the praise and glory, cherishing and pondering these things in her heart.

There are so many lessons we need to learn from Mary—to re-examine the qualities we choose to admire in others and make room to admire the quiet and understated beauty of faithful and gentle spirits, to reflect on whether our own characters are marked by humility and obedience, and to ask for God's help in remembering that we are not the heroes of the story at all.

PRAYER & REFLECTION

* Have you lost sight that this season—and our very lives—are really all about Jesus? Ask God to help you reorient your heart to this reality.
* Spend some time reflecting upon the words of Mary (paraphrased below). Make them your own prayer:

  Lord, I am your servant. I am ready to be and
  do whatever you will.

DECEMBER 15

Where Joy is Found

The Lord is my strength and my shield;
my heart trusts in him, and he helps me.
My heart leaps for joy,
and with my song I praise him.

PSALM 28:7

Happiness is the siren of our lives. We set goals in pursuit of the seductive hope that *it* can be obtained. We dream of earthly rewards—the admiration of our peers, financial security, influence and status—though in our modern age, nothing is treasured more highly than the idols of self-actualisation and "true love" (by which we generally mean romantic or sexual fulfillment). Who can claim that such siren-songs are without impact on their hearts?

The sirens of Greek mythology are a useful parable for us. These beautiful strangers were alluring at a distance. Sailors longed to obtain them, changing course, ignoring the readings of their navigational instruments. But the result of all this was heartbreak as well as shipwreck—because the sirens were never what they seemed.

You and I are on a journey. We know where our focus should be and we're equipped—through God's word, the indwelling of the Holy Spirit, and the community of the faithful—to remain on track. We *know* that true joy, true love, true belonging and true meaning are all to be found in our Lord... and yet we can hear that siren-song as we travel on our way.

To be tempted to pursue our own ends is human

nature. To fall off the path and have to course-correct is something we've all experienced at some point—some of us many times. But in his mercy, our Lord provides us with encouraging glimpses of the true joy that awaits us, glimpses that make the earth's songs fall flat.

The human heroes of the Bible had sirens of their own. We know this much, even if we don't know all of the details about their particular struggles. Scripture tells us what we *need* to know. Sometimes this includes witnessing moments of cringe-worthy failure, but at other times we get to witness moments of life-changing joy. Luke's gospel opens with a series of such moments. Mary, Zechariah, Simeon, and the very angels of heaven, were all caught up in the wonder and delight of the incarnation. The irrepressible praise of God sprang from each in turn, welling up and overflowing in song as they caught a glimpse of what God was doing.

Mary had been visited by the angel Gabriel, and was filled with wonder at the role she'd been chosen to play. She went to visit Elizabeth, who was pregnant with John the Baptist, and who welcomed her with this Spirit-filled exclamation:

> "Blessed are you among women, and blessed is the child you will bear! But why am I so favoured, that the mother of my Lord should come to me? As soon as the sound of your greeting reached my ears, the baby in my womb leaped for joy. Blessed is she who has believed that the Lord would fulfill his promises to her" (LUKE 1: 42-45)!

The baby leaped for joy. Elizabeth's heart was full of gladness and gratitude. And Mary sang praises to God for his goodness, not just to her, but to every generation that would place its trust in him.

Happiness versus joy. One entices us to focus on self-interest, the other enlarges our vision with the perspective of eternity, equipping us to reach our ultimate destination, whatever we might encounter on the way.

Both Elizabeth and Mary were given special sons—sons who would die violent deaths at the hands of unjust men. God's good and gracious plan was not for their earthly comfort, but for *our* eternal salvation. Elizabeth and Mary had the precious joy of knowing that God was at work. In the years that were to come, only such joy, drawn from such a source, could sustain them.

PRAYER & REFLECTION

* Is your life characterised by gratitude and contentment? Or has the pursuit of elusive, earthly "happiness" distracted you from the source of true joy? Ask God to help you course-correct.
* Set aside some time to read through Mary's song of praise (LUKE 1:46-55) (below). Note how these verses point to the source of Mary's joy:

> My soul glorifies the Lord, and my spirit rejoices in God my Saviour, for he has been mindful of the humble state of his servant. From now on all generations will call me blessed, for the Mighty One has done great things for me—holy is his name.
>
> His mercy extends to those who fear him, from generation to generation. He has performed mighty deeds with his arm; he has scattered those who are proud in their inmost thoughts. He has brought down rulers from their thrones but has lifted up the humble. He has filled the hungry with good things but has sent the rich away empty. He has helped his servant Israel, remembering to be merciful to Abraham and his descendants forever, just as he promised our ancestors.

DECEMBER 16

The Great Wedding

"Let us rejoice and be glad and give him glory!
For the wedding of the Lamb has come,
and his bride has made herself ready."

REVELATION 19:7

The search for "true love" occupies a lot of space in our culture. The restless longing in each of us, the "God-shaped hole" within, yearns for something we don't fully understand. Our world believes that this universal longing can be satisfied through human romance, but believers across the centuries have argued that it can be met only by the lover of our souls. We were made *by* and *for* God. How could we ever find fulfillment apart from him?

The season of Advent *rumbles* with the anticipation of a great wedding. Have you noticed?

The Old Testament prophets spoke of God's faithful spousal love for his people. The book of Isaiah says, "your Maker is your husband" (54:5), and in the book of the prophet Hosea, the Lord speaks these words to Israel:

> "In that day, you will call me 'my husband'; you will no longer call me 'my master...' I will betroth you to me forever; I will betroth you in righteousness and justice, in love and compassion. I will betroth you in faithfulness..." (HOSEA 2:16,19-20).

The Lord's love for his people is a husband's love. This is not a *metaphor* for true husband-love—it is its *archetype*. In the same way that good parents emulate the fatherhood of God, good marriages emulate his passionate devotion. Throughout the pages of the Old Testament we see how undeserving human beings are, and yet how gracious the Lord is. We have hurt and betrayed him, and he has rescued and redeemed us. We are his betrothed, and he has not given up on us. In spite of all our failures, he will ensure that the promised wedding day comes. *Rumble.*

When John the Baptist arrived on the scene, he called himself a "friend of the Bridegroom" (JOHN 3:29). He understood that he was merely a herald announcing the arrival of the one who had come to claim the bride. Jesus also spoke of himself as the Bridegroom, and his sacrificial love is the biblical model for Christian husbands:

> Husbands, love your wives, just as Christ loved the church and gave himself up for her to make her holy, cleansing her by the washing with water through the word, and to present her to himself as a radiant church... (EPHESIANS 5:25-27).

Believers today live in an awkward in-between moment. The Bridegroom has come. He has sacrificed himself for us, and our future with him has been secured. The Holy Spirit is with us, sanctifying us, making us ready. But while all of this is true, our hearts—and creation itself—are longing for what's still to come. *Rumble.*

The parables and epistles speak to us with words of encouragement as well as warning. The future we await is glorious beyond imagining, but in the meantime we must be alert and faithful. Though the waiting can be hard, we have joy in knowing how the story will end. *Rumble.*

The traditional music of Advent,[3] calls us to reflect

---

[3] *The hymns and carols of Advent are not the same as those of Christmas, which in many settings have displaced the traditional music of Advent. Further details can be found in the resource section of this book, see page 124.*

upon eschatological (end times) themes, and especially upon the epic romance that we've been caught up in:

> The watchers on the mountain
> Proclaim the Bridegroom near;
> Go meet him as he cometh,
> With hallelujahs clear.
> The marriage feast is waiting,
> The gates wide open stand!
> Up, up, ye heirs of glory,
> The Bridegroom is at hand![4]

Advent looks back at the promises we've received and at all that our Lord has done for us, but it also looks ahead with anticipation to his return. It reminds us powerfully that the "not yet" of our present circumstances will soon be swallowed up in victory and true fulfillment:

> In thy presence is fullness of joy; at thy right hand there are pleasures for evermore (PSALM 16:11, KJV).

The way has been made for us, and the best is yet to come. The long-awaited day is coming soon. *Rumble, rumble, rumble.* Do you have goosebumps yet?

PRAYER & REFLECTION

* When you think about God's love for his people, do you consider it in the light of his spousal love? Why or why not? How might this add depth to your understanding? Take some time to reflect on this now.
* Does the example of our Lord's faithful and sacrificial love impact your attitude towards marriage (and if you are married, your participation in that covenant)? How might this become a greater part of your witness to a world that desperately needs to know God's love?

---

[4] *Quoted from the hymn "Rejoice All Ye Believers," see page 137 for full text.*

DECEMBER 17

Dark Night of the Soul

When John, who was in prison, heard about the deeds of the Messiah, he sent his disciples to ask him, "Are you the one who is to come, or should we expect someone else?"

MATTHEW 11:2-3

This is a passage of scripture to break the heart. The fiery preacher, the last of the Old Testament-era prophets, the great forerunner of the Messiah—steeped in darkness and doubt, plunged into a dark night of the soul.

John the Baptist's father had received a sign from an angel. His mother had learned first-hand from Mary about the annunciation. John himself had "lived rough," preaching God's word boldly and lambasting religious leaders for their hypocrisy. He'd prophesied about Jesus, baptised him, and heard the voice from heaven declare *who* this was. But now there's a question nagging at John's mind.

What happened here? How could faith and zeal like that of the baptist-prophet become a fog of uncertainty?

John was no longer in the wilderness carrying out a ministry that drew people from across the region. Instead, he was in Herod's dungeon. He would die there, his ministry ended by an immoral tyrant. Was *this* really God's plan?

Was this really God's plan? How many believers, you and I included, have asked that question over the years?

Every one of us experiences crises of faith. Disappointments, tragedies, unmet expectations—all can plunge us into a season of disillusionment and soul-searching.

There can be a tendency among us to look down on those experiencing a crisis of faith, as though this were a divine judgement or a sign of spiritual weakness. But Jesus did not respond to John with a rebuke, nor did he criticise him. Scripture tells us that trials and temptations come to all of us, and that such times can be instruments of grace, refining fires that help bring us to spiritual maturity:

> These trials have come so that the proven genuineness of your faith—of greater worth than gold, which perishes even though refined by fire—may result in praise, glory and honour when Jesus Christ is revealed (1 PETER 1:7).

In times of doubt and discouragement, we must choose how we respond. There are two major traps we can fall prey to. The first is to deny the struggle we are experiencing—smiling, lying, going through the motions, never acknowledging the truth about the darkness we are facing, never humbling ourselves to seek the support and encouragement of fellow believers. The second trap, which is especially popular in modern times, is to "deconstruct." We can reject all that we've believed, reject the authority of the one who saved us, and seek to find within ourselves some new authority with which to build a more convenient worldview. Neither of these responses will lead us through our crisis to spiritual maturity in Christ.

We can learn a great deal from John's example. He did not *deny* his crisis, nor did he *deconstruct* his faith. Instead, he held firm to his confidence in God's promise, though he questioned his own understanding of it. He humbled himself and addressed his question to the one with the authority to answer it.

Jesus understood completely. His response was not condemning, nor dismissive, but encouraging. He pointed to the promise of scripture. And he affirmed what John already knew in his heart, but needed to hear:

> "Go back and report to John what you hear and see: The blind receive sight, the lame walk, those who have leprosy are cleansed, the deaf hear, the dead are raised, and the good news is proclaimed to the poor..." (MATTHEW 11:4-5).

There's something else that stands out about Jesus' response to John. *The answer is in his actions.* Jesus' answer is more than mere words, perhaps because the question itself also runs deeper than words. *Was Jesus really the Messiah? Was this how it was supposed to go? Was God still in control? Was the ultimate outcome still sure?* Jesus could have simply said "Yes," but instead he pointed to all of the signs which John already knew by heart, and confirmed that it was so.

Dark nights come to each of us when the questions crowd in. *Was this really how it was supposed to go? Why didn't God intervene? Does he even care?* Each time we find ourselves asking these questions, the answer is there in his actions. He humbled himself to take on human flesh *for us*. He suffered and died *for us*. He is making a home in heaven *for us*. *There* is our answer.

PRAYER & REFLECTION

* What crises have you faced in your spiritual life? How did you respond to them? If there are unresolved struggles in your heart, ask the Lord to guide you through these dark nights till you reach his side in glory.
* Are there others known to you who are struggling? Uphold them in prayer and consider how you might be a support and encouragement to them.

Week Four

COME, LORD JESUS

He who testifies to these things says,
"Yes, I am coming soon."
Amen. Come, Lord Jesus.

REVELATION 22:20

DECEMBER 18

Maranatha

At that time they will see the Son of Man coming in a cloud with power and great glory. When these things begin to take place, stand up and lift up your heads, because your redemption is drawing near.

LUKE 21:27-28

What goes through your mind when you hear the words "end times"? Does the phrase fill you with zeal, or perhaps make you wary? Many Christians today tend to fall into two extremes when eschatological[1] topics arise. We can either become dogmatic and combative about our theological positions, or with a sense of deep embarrassment we can avoid the topic entirely. Neither of these responses is helpful. On the one hand, scripture clearly tells us that some things are known only to the Father (MATTHEW 24:36*ff.*), and on the other hand, we are instructed to keep watch, and to encourage one another with the assurance of the wonderful things still to come (1 THESSALONIANS 4:18).

The Nicene creed models an excellent balance for us. What is this creed? Well, briefly, it was written by the leaders of the Church in the fourth century to clarify essential Christian doctrine, and it is still considered authoritative across denominational lines today. This statement of faith doesn't get caught up with squabbling over details that

---

1 *"Eschatology" refers to doctrines concerning the last things or the end times, including the second coming of Jesus, the resurrection of the dead, the judgment of humanity, and eternal life (heaven/hell). It also includes doctrines related to the rapture, tribulation, millennialism, and the end of the world.*

we cannot hope to fully grasp, but neither does it avoid speaking with clear confidence about those truths which bind Christians together:

> I believe... Jesus Christ... shall come again with glory to judge both the quick [living] and the dead: whose kingdom shall have no end... and I look for the resurrection of the dead, and the life of the world to come.[2]

Eschatology matters. It matters because it is these beliefs that assure us things will not go on as they are forever. We live in a paradoxical moment in time. On the one hand, we have already received the fulfillment of God's promised redemption in Jesus; we've been sent the Holy Spirit; together, believers form the Body of Christ. But on the other hand, Jesus' return has not yet happened—and while we work and wait, there's sin and suffering all around. Eschatology reminds us that there is an urgency to the work that we do here because time is limited; but more than this, it gives us hope in knowing that we are destined for more than the hardships and limitations of this life.

Eschatology was immensely important to early Christians. It shaped their belief, their worship and their social culture. Whereas the traditional greeting of the Old Testament had been *"shalom"* ("peace" in Hebrew), the early Church believers adopted the Aramaic greeting *"maranatha."* This greeting translates as both a petition ("Come, O Lord") and also an affirmation ("The Lord is coming"), and it rooted believers in the hope and expectation of Christ's return. In the modern Church it is no longer the custom to greet one another in this way—and our sense of urgency, our hope and expectation, often pales in comparison to those early believers.

Eschatology also matters because without it we cannot

[2] *Quoted from the Nicene Creed (Book of Common Prayer translation).*

begin to grasp *who Jesus is*. There is much we come to understand about Jesus from reading about his life and ministry on earth, but this is not the whole picture. Jesus is co-eternal with the Father. He was present and active in the creation of the world. He will return in power and glory, and will reign forever. This is the cosmic king, the one who is "the same, yesterday, today and forever" (HEBREWS 13:8). And this is the picture-behind-the-picture of the suffering servant, the humble carpenter, the baby in the manger.

As Christmas draws near, we begin to greet one another with the words "Merry Christmas," and our hearts rightly rejoice because of the baby who was like no other baby. But we need *more* than the message of Christmas. We need the reminders that Easter and Pentecost bring—and we need the spirit of Advent to prompt our hearts to say to one another again, "Maranatha!"

PRAYER & REFLECTION

* What is your usual response to end times topics? Do you need to shift your focus away from either avoidance or combativeness? Ask God to reshape your perspective and attitude.
* Does the hope of the Lord's return have a place in your heart? Reflect on the word "maranatha," and ask God to make this your heart's cry.
* Finally, take some time to read prayerfully through the following hymn lyrics. Ask God to ignite within you a spirit of adoration for his beloved Son.

> Yea, amen; let all adore thee,
> High on thine eternal throne;
> Saviour, take the power and glory;
> Claim the kingdoms for thine own:
> Alleluia! Thou shalt reign, and thou alone![3]

[3] *Quoted from "Lo, he comes with clouds descending," full text on page 131.*

DECEMBER 19

Sapientia

Through Jesus, let us continually offer to God a sacrifice of praise—the fruit of lips that openly profess his name.

HEBREWS 13:15

In an ancient Christian monastery, sometime during the 8th or 9th century, a beautiful hymn was penned. It was written in Latin and sung as a simple chant. Then, a thousand years later, this hymn was translated into English and expanded into what we know today as "O Come, O Come, Emmanuel." But the old Latin hymn took *its* inspiration from a still older tradition, referred to simply as the "O Antiphons."[4]

Picture the monks in their chapel, praying and singing and reading from the scriptures, many times each day. Their evening prayers are always punctuated by the recitation of the *Magnificat*—Mary's Song (LUKE 1:46-55). But in the last days of Advent, with Christmas just around the corner, the monks have added something special to this discipline. There is a sung prayer, an "antiphon," repeated before and after the *Magnificat*. Each day's antiphon is different, forming a set of meditations on the person of Christ, based on seven Messianic titles: *Wisdom, Lord, Root of Jesse, Key of David, Dayspring, King of the Nations, God With Us.*

In the days which remain until Christmas Eve, we'll use these ancient antiphon-prayers to stir us to marvel at the mystery and greatness of God's plan in the person of

[4] *Further details can be found in the resource section, page 149.*

Jesus—much as our spiritual ancestors have done across centuries and continents.

*

The first of the O Antiphons addresses Jesus as "Sapientia" *(Latin)*—that is, "Wisdom." This is not the best known of our Lord's titles, though it comes to us from the familiar Messianic prophecies of Isaiah:

> The spirit of the Lord shall rest upon him: a spirit of wisdom and of understanding, a spirit of counsel and of strength, a spirit of knowledge and fear of the Lord, and his delight shall be the fear of the Lord (ISAIAH 11:2-3).

When we begin to explore the wisdom of Jesus, we find that the subject runs very deep. How exactly do we define wisdom? In what way does Jesus embody this trait? And how does all of this relate to us? Let's (very briefly) tackle these questions in order.

How do we define wisdom? The foundation of biblical wisdom is "the fear of the Lord" (PROVERBS 9:10)—but what does this mean? This *fear* is all about our posture before the one who created us, the omnipotent God of the universe. It's about recognising our smallness and unworthiness as his creatures. Rather than rejecting his authority in a spirit of pride-fuelled autonomy as we are so often tempted to do, "fearing him" is about a reverent acknowledgment of who he is, and living life in that light.

Jesus' ability to embody this holy wisdom was unique. He was "the Word;" it was his role to "go forth" from the Father to accomplish his will (ISAIAH 55:11). As such, Jesus was active in creation, a teacher of teachers, and master over nature. He was equipped for his mission with knowledge and power. And he had authority—to heal, to forgive, to speak and to send in the Father's name. He will return, triumphant, to reign. But in spite of all this, Jesus' earthly ministry was marked by humility and submission; his every step aligned to the Father's plan and timing. Though he was "in very nature God," he did not seek to have his own way, but "humbled himself" (PHILIPPIANS 2:6-8), taking on the helplessness and weakness of a human infant, suffering and dying as a man. "With humility comes wisdom" (PROVERBS 11:2), and Jesus is our example in this.

Those who seek to be wise must begin with the fear of the Lord and look to the example of Christ's humility. But we must also reclaim a virtue which has fallen out of fashion in modern times, a virtue which many of the saints of Church history considered the strength and support of all the others—*prudence*. Prudence is defined as thoughtful caution, discernment, discipline and good judgement. And this is what it takes to cultivate a spirit of humility; to train our hearts and minds to walk in obedience; to seek our Lord's face, to listen for his voice, and to revere his will. And so, we pray with the words of the first O Antiphon:

> O Wisdom, coming forth from the mouth of the Most High, reaching from one end of the heavens to the other, mightily and sweetly ordering all things: Come and teach us the way of prudence.

PRAYER & REFLECTION

* Using the words of the ancient antiphon as a "springboard" (see above), take some time to reflect upon Jesus' role as the Wisdom of the Most High. Close your time with a prayerful consideration of the need for prudence in your life, and in the life of the Church.
* Commit yourself anew to be led by the Wisdom of God, and to be urged on and corrected by his Word.

DECEMBER 20

Adonai

Indeed the Lord will be there with us, majestic;
yes the Lord our judge, the Lord our lawgiver,
the Lord our king, he it is who will save us.

ISAIAH 33:22

Our world is full of authority figures. Police officers and school teachers, judges and monarchs, all have jurisdictions in which respectful compliance is appropriate. There are words we use to show respect in how we address those in such positions: *Officer, Sir, Your Honour, Your Majesty.* But how do we speak of one whose authority is much greater than these frail placeholders? How do we address one who is sovereign over all of creation?

The Old Testament makes frequent use of the word "Adonai" *(Hebrew)*, which is usually translated as "Lord." It refers to someone in authority, someone who is to be respected and obeyed. Though human authorities can never—in their own right—deserve to be addressed in this way, there *is* one to whom we owe total allegiance. This is the authority behind the very idea of authority. This is the one we must obey.

Obedience. How do you feel about this word? Does it give rise to rebellious impulses in you? If so, you're not alone. The history of the human race is a story of *dis*obedience. The first man and woman disobeyed in the garden. Those who received the law on Sinai never did keep it. The Apostle Paul described the experience which is common to each of us with the words, "what I want to do I do not do, but what I hate I do" (ROMANS 7:15). Though we may address God as "Lord" with our lips, our lives are littered with evidence of our inability to consistently honour him as Lord.

The "first Adam," our ancestor, was disobedient. Down through the ages, we all have inherited the legacy of sin and death (ROMANS 5:12). Jesus came to be the "second Adam," to give us a new legacy, a legacy of life and freedom, rooted in joyful obedience (1 CORINTHIANS 15:45).

Jesus' incarnation, his earthly life, epitomised obedience. The Lord of all came in obedience, walked in obedience, died in obedience. He showed us what obedience looks like. *He* was obedient because *we* never have been. When faced with temptations in the wilderness, Jesus quoted the words of scripture, and did not yield. The prayer he taught was centred around holy submission to the Father (*"Your will be done,"* MATTHEW 6:10). And in Gethsemane, with the crucifixion before him, Jesus again committed himself to surrender to the will of the Father (*"Not my will, but yours be done,"* LUKE 22:42).

Our God is the sovereign lawgiver, the one who must be obeyed. But he is also the one who designed our redemption. And Jesus Christ, God the Son, came in obedience to fulfill all that was required. The second of the O Antiphons, *Adonai,* invites us to reflect on these things:

> O Adonai, and ruler of the house of Israel,
> who appeared to Moses in the burning bush,
> and gave him the law on Sinai: Come and re-
> deem us with an outstretched arm!

Come and redeem us. Jesus our redeemer *has* come. He came as a baby, but he did not stay a baby. And where is the humble child of Bethlehem now? He is seated at the right hand of God the Father, interceding for us. He is preparing to return as king and judge. Jesus, the one who came in humility and modelled obedience for us, is Adonai, the sovereign Lord, whose authority *we* must obey.

The book of Revelation gives us this awe-inspiring picture of our Lord Jesus Christ:

> His eyes were like blazing fire... his voice was like the sound of rushing waters... his face was like the sun shining in all its brilliance... Then he... said: "Do not be afraid. I am the First and the Last. I am the Living One; I was dead, and now look, I am alive for ever and ever! And I hold the keys of death and Hades..." (REVELATION 1:12-18).

As we prepare to adore the baby in a manger, we remember that this baby is Lord of all. He is the conquerer of death. He is the long-awaited Messiah, and our deliverer. He is the true prophet, priest, and king; our mediator and advocate in heaven. Jesus our sovereign Lord is everything to us. He is the inspiration for the songs we sing. He is our heart's cry. And when we fix our eyes on him and all that he has done, we find the encouragement we need to follow after his example in loving, grateful obedience.

PRAYER & REFLECTION

* Using the words of the ancient antiphon as a "springboard" (see previous page), take some time to reflect upon the Lordship of Jesus Christ.
* Choose one of the following verses to contemplate and pray with:

> "Our Father in heaven, hallowed be your name, your kingdom come, *your will be done*, on earth as it is in heaven" (MATTHEW 6:9-10).

> "Father, if you are willing, take this cup from me; yet *not my will, but yours be done*" (LUKE 22:42).

DECEMBER 21

Shepherd of Shepherds

This is the genealogy of Jesus the Messiah,
the son of David, the son of Abraham...

MATTHEW 1:1

Genealogies tend to confuse and bore us. Why should scripture even include such lists? What do they matter? What do they mean? That they *do* mean something is demonstrated by the fact that they *are* included. They serve the purpose of drawing our eye backwards to historic people and events; they highlight and illuminate; they connect dots across centuries that begin to form a picture.

The genealogy of Jesus prompts us to reflect upon the story of our salvation—as we've already been doing throughout Advent. These verses touch upon the call of Abraham, and the faith and failures present in each generation. They remind us of God's willingness to work in and through flawed human beings, and his redemptive grace in drawing Gentiles into his family. But most of all, *this* genealogy reverberates with God's promise to provide a true Shepherd to lead his flock to their eternal home.

The third and fourth of the O Antiphons[5] zoom in on two names in the genealogy of Jesus—Jesse and David. The Old Testament prophets promised that a descendant of these men would one day come to save, to lead, and to

[5] *O Radix Jesse (O Root of Jesse) and O Clavis David (O Key of David)—see page 151 of the resource section for more details.*

establish a kingdom of peace and justice under his perfect care and authority. But as we look back, we are also powerfully reminded that no human leader, not even David the shepherd-king, has ever been a truly *good* shepherd.

Down through the centuries, human leaders entrusted to lead God's flock have always done so under God's authority, and they are answerable to him, the Shepherd of shepherds. Many men and women have been raised up to lead God's people. Some strive to serve faithfully. But both scripture and Church history are filled with examples of bad shepherds and outright wolves—leaders who cause more harm than good, who lead the sheep away from the true Shepherd through false teaching or immoral practice, who exploit the sheep for their own gain. Even among those shepherds who humbly seek to emulate the one great Shepherd, none can do so perfectly.

Jesus came to be the true good Shepherd. He was born among the livestock, placed in a manger, and worshipped by shepherds. He lived in the midst of the ones he came to save; he walked in the dirt, and often had "no place to lay his head" (MATTHEW 8:20). During his earthly ministry, Jesus looked out over the crowds and "had compassion on them, because they were harassed and helpless, like sheep without a shepherd" (MATTHEW 9:36). He knew what they needed: a shepherd who would not abuse his flock, but would sacrifice himself to keep them safe. Jesus said, "I am the good shepherd. The good shepherd lays down his life for the sheep" (JOHN 10:11).

The Shepherd of shepherds came to be a sacrificial lamb. Only in this way could he lead us through the dark valleys of this world and on to that home where we will dwell with him forever:

> "Never again will they hunger; never again will they thirst. The sun will not beat down

> on them," nor any scorching heat. For the Lamb at the centre of the throne will be their shepherd; "he will lead them to springs of living water." "And God will wipe away every tear from their eyes" (REVELATION 7:16-17).

This is where the journey leads. And this great Shepherd is the only one who can lead us there.

When gifted leaders arise among us, we must give thanks for them and uphold them in prayer. But we must keep our eyes fixed on Jesus, with our hope and our faith rooted in him alone. When human leaders betray our confidence, and when we find ourselves crying with exasperation, "Who is worthy of trust?"—Jesus is the answer. He is the Shepherd who will never exploit us, who will never lead us astray. Every step we take on this journey of life is taken under his providential care. He has sacrificed himself for us; he has "engraved" us on the palms of his hands (ISAIAH 49:16). And the nail-pierced hands of the good Shepherd are worthy of our whole-hearted trust.

PRAYER & REFLECTION

* Have you been hurt or disappointed by Christian leaders? Take a moment to bring the matter before God. Ask him to help you respect and support human leaders in accordance with his will, but to place all your hope and assurance in the only truly good Shepherd.
* Slowly read through the following passage. Take some time for worship and thanksgiving.

> Jesus said, "My sheep listen to my voice; I know them, and they follow me. I give them eternal life, and they shall never perish; no one will snatch them out of my hand" (JOHN 10:27-28).

DECEMBER 22

Light Eternal

Jesus said, "I am the light of the world.
Whoever follows me will never walk in darkness,
but will have the light of life."

JOHN 8:12

Here, in the northern hemisphere, we've entered the darkest part of the year. Our days are short. Months of winter, cold and barren, stretch out before us, and many of us feel the emotional darkness of stress or sadness closing in. We need a supernatural light to carry us through.

The fifth O Antiphon ("O Oriens," *Latin*) addresses our Lord as the source of light that we need so desperately:

> O Dayspring, Splendour of Light Eternal and Sun of Righteousness: Come and give light to those who dwell in darkness and the shadow of death.

This grouping of titles for Jesus is rich with scriptural allusion, and each one is worthy of contemplation. But today, we're just going to look briefly at four ways that Jesus' light delivers us from darkness and shadow.

Jesus is the light that leads us into truth. The darkness of our world—and of our minds—is marked by ignorance, pride, sin and error. Each of these things blinds us to the truth about the one who loves us, and creates obstacles to our accepting the truth of the gospel. But God is not deterred by the difficulty of the task; his plan of redemption is able to break through every barrier: Jesus was born, eternity entered time, immortality took on frailty. The crucifixion of the Saviour seemed like a catastrophe, but it wasn't one. Instead, it was the means of atoning for our sin, and set the stage for the victory of the resurrection.

God works in mysterious ways and is willing to go to great lengths to reach us. Consider the magi. These men were not observant Jews. Their inadequate understanding prompted them to search the stars for insight into earthly events. In spite of this God did not write them off; he did not wait for them to stumble into a synagogue before reaching out to them. As he does with each of us, he met them in their sin and error. He spoke in a language they could understand. And he led them to Jesus, the true light of the world.

The light of Jesus' presence illuminates our journey. There are times when the darkness closes in and we feel lost and alone. But those who belong to Jesus are neither lost nor alone. We've been given the indwelling Holy Spirit to comfort and guide us. We are in the trustworthy hands of the Saviour every moment of our lives. He has promised to be with us "to the very end of the age" (MATTHEW 28:20), giving us "joy unspeakable" (1 PETER 1:8 KJV), peace that "transcends all understanding" (PHILIPPIANS 4:7), and hope like an "anchor for the soul, firm and secure" (HEBREWS 6:19). Whatever we may *feel*, this remains constant and true.

The light of Christ is ours to share. Though we may sometimes wish that God would simply take us home to heaven, there is a reason for us to be here now. He has commissioned us to participate in the work of sharing his light. We have a purpose, a mission. We're here to be "salt and light," preserving what is good and countering what is evil (MATTHEW 5:13-16). We're here to be "ambassadors," calling others out of the darkness, and introducing them to the Saviour (2 CORINTHIANS 5:20)—and the time we have is limited.

The light will triumph, and darkness will be no more. The book of Revelation tells us this about the heavenly city:

> The city does not need the sun or the moon to shine on it, for the glory of God gives it light, and the Lamb is its lamp. The nations will walk by its light, and the kings of the earth will bring their splendour into it. On no day will its gates ever be shut, for there will be no night there (REVELATION 21:23-25).

Whenever the Bible provides us with glimpses of heaven, it's apparent that much of it is beyond our grasp. But some things we do understand. We understand that we will be with our Saviour and Lord, and all the darknesses of this fallen world will be ancient history. The joy, peace, and love that we can now only taste on the tip of our tongue, will then be the defining reality of our existence.

Whether or not there is snow on the ground where you are, whether or not your days have gotten shorter, the questions still remain. How will you make it through the winter? Through a difficult season of life? Through until the end? You *can* and *will* make it through by holding fast to the one who can illuminate the path for you. In this light, you can look backwards and see that his goodness and love have been pursuing you all the way. In this light, you can know you are not alone. In this light, you can find purpose and joy in helping others along the road. And in this light, one day, the darkness—whatever form your particular darkness takes—will be forever banished.

PRAYER & REFLECTION

* What form of darkness confronts you as you consider the season ahead? Spend some time reflecting upon Jesus, the Light Eternal—who saves us, accompanies us, commissions us, and awaits us in glory.
* Take a few minutes to pray, using the words of the ancient antiphon (see page 87).

DECEMBER 23

King of the Nations

Then the Lord God formed a man from the dust of the ground and breathed into his nostrils the breath of life, and the man became a living being.

GENESIS 2:7

Dust and divine breath. This is where the story began for us. All of humanity shares this point of origin. We have a common Creator. We are made of the same stuff. But in spite of this, all human beings do not belong to the same family, not anymore.

Family. It's a word we use a lot. It speaks to our sense of identity and belonging. Whereas once it mainly described blood ties, we now often use it to describe those people we are most at home with, perhaps our friends or a community with shared experiences. However we choose to define family, it is something we all long for.

At their best, families can provide a sense of safety, a solid foundation where growth is nurtured and love overflows to show hospitality to outsiders, inviting them in. But the larger human family, and many families within it, are distortions of what they might have been in Eden.

That larger human family, through which we all trace our ancestry, is a dysfunctional one. We are all born into sin, born into a state of rebellion and estrangement. We are hostile prodigals who have disowned our loving Father. We are not the heirs we were created to be.

Jesus, when he became incarnate, entered into the midst of this dysfunction. We often picture the tableau of

Mary and Joseph and the baby, wholesome and holy. But the human race Jesus came into the midst of was anything but wholesome and holy. Jesus was born into the same world that we are born into: filled with cruelty and grief, with vice and suffering, with sin and death.

Jesus became part of the dysfunctional human race so that we could be adopted into a new family. With his blood he "purchased for God persons from every tribe and language and people and nation" (REVELATION 5:9). Through the shedding of Jesus' blood, our old blood ties are broken, and new ones are established.

This brings us to the sixth and penultimate O Antiphon—"Rex Gentium" (*Latin*), or "King of the Nations":

> O King of the Nations, and their desire; O Cornerstone making both one: Come and save the human race, which you made from the dust of the earth.

Regardless of backstory, ethnicity, family structure, or sinful propensities, the way to true belonging is open to all. Jesus *has* come to save us. Through him, we enter this new family alongside others who are completely unlike ourselves. We come from different parts of the world, we look different, we speak different languages, we have different life experiences—but we have in common the one thing that matters more than any other—we accept Jesus as Saviour, and acknowledge him as King.

This new family is our forever family. We will spend eternity with them in heaven, reunited with the Father who created us and the Brother-King who has done so much to bring us home. Jesus talked about it this way:

> "My Father's house has many rooms; if that were not so, would I have told you that I am going there to prepare a place for you? And if I go and prepare a place for you, I will come

> back and take you to be with me that you also may be where I am" (JOHN 14:2-3).

Because of what Jesus has done, we are now heirs of eternity. We now have a new family. And we now have a calling that flows out of these gifts. We are to love this family and the brothers and sisters who belong to it with a special love. Jesus said, "By this everyone will know that you are my disciples, if you love one another" (JOHN 13:35). This brother-love is not always evident among believers, but it is what we are called to. It is part of our witness.

The love that we've been shown, the family blessings that have been showered upon us, are not just meant to flow into love for one another, but they are meant to *over*flow. The homes and churches that we build here can be an earthly foretaste of our eternal home. They can be places where brother-love witnesses to the greater brother-love that Jesus has shown for us. We can be a people who invite outsiders in—to experience this love, this unity, this wholesome, holy family that we were made for, and that we will one day come home to.

PRAYER & REFLECTION

* What are your family associations? Have you been blessed with a wholesome and loving Christian home? Seek the Lord's help in honouring the good gift he's given, and in hospitably sharing it with others. Are you distressed by the inadequacies of the human family that surrounds you? Remember that you have been adopted into an eternal family, and ask your Father-King to give you a deep assurance that you belong to him. Then, ask him to help you to follow his example in showing love to the dysfunctional people you live among.

DECEMBER 24

Emmanuel

Your life is now hidden with Christ in God. When Christ, who is your life, appears, then you also will appear with him in glory.

COLOSSIANS 3:3-4

The O Antiphons come to us from an age much closer to the time in which the New Testament was written. This was a time when persecution of Christians was severe and widespread; a time when Christians used the secret symbol of a fish[6] to reveal their faith in Jesus Christ; a time when the expectation of the Lord's immanent return was palpable in every greeting of "Maranatha." So, it should not surprise us that the monastic authors of the O Antiphons layered further meaning in these prayers with a reverse acrostic in the original Latin:

O Sapientia (O Wisdom)
O Adonai (O Lord)
O Radix Jesse (O Root of Jesse)
O Clavis David (O Key of David)
O Oriens (O Dayspring)
O Rex Gentium (O King of the Nations)
O Emmanuel (O God With Us)

The first letter of each title together spells out *ERO CRAS*—a Latin phrase which means "Tomorrow I am coming."

Two thousand years on from the events of the New

[6] *Early Christians used a fish symbol to identify one another. The word* fish *in Greek* (ichthys) *forms an acronym for the phrase "Jesus Christ, Son of God, Saviour."*

Testament finds us in a different mood. Many of us are more comfortable and feel less urgency regarding our Lord's return. And yet our need for the presence of such a divine friend is unabated. We struggle to find meaning and belonging, to be truly known and loved, to have some assurance that we are not alone and adrift in the darkness of this world.

The friend we need, the friend who "sticks closer than a brother" (PROVERBS 18:24), is the same friend who walked with our spiritual ancestors. He walked with those who held fast—for generations—to the promise of a Messiah. He said, "I will never leave you, nor forsake you" (DEUTERONOMY 31:6)—and he didn't. He walked with those who wept at the foot of his cross, grief-stricken and confused at how this could really be God's plan. He knew what it was to weep, and he is able to empathise with our weakness (HEBREWS 4:15). He walked with the persecuted believers of the early Church. He said, "where two or three gather in my name, there am I with them" (MATTHEW 18:20)—and so he has been down through the centuries.

We need this friend—this friend who the prophet Isaiah called "Emmanuel" *(Hebrew)*, which means *God with us*. It is in him we find meaning for our lives. In him we are truly known and loved—he has seen us at our worst, and would still give everything to rescue us. In him we have assurance that we are neither alone nor adrift. In him we find our destiny, our hope, our true love, our eternal home.

How did this best of friends come to us? How was this unfathomable miracle brought into our world?

God's ways are beyond us. This much is clear. Who could have imagined such a salvation and such a Saviour? Who would have dared to suggest that the one who carries such titles—Mighty God, Prince of Peace, King of the Nations—should take on human flesh, be born into obscurity and hardship—and with such a path to tread, such a cup to drink?

On this eve of Christmas, whether you feel yourself to be surrounded by earthly blessings or whether you feel your blessings to be few, set aside those thoughts and concerns long enough to remember what it is that we are celebrating: God's loving plan to bring you home to himself, through the gift of Jesus Christ.

All of this, all that we have been reflecting on during the season of Advent, it is all *for you*. It cannot be contained in garlands or shiny parcels. It cannot be adequately distilled in music. Whether you celebrate with feasting in a fine house surrounded by family, or whether you celebrate in scarcity, ultimately makes no difference. The Lord Jesus "dropped down from heaven," breaking into human history, taking on human flesh—to rescue *you*, to make you an heir of salvation, and to prepare your forever home with him in heaven. *Gloria in excelsis Deo!* Glory to God in the highest!

PRAYER & REFLECTION

* On this eve of Christmas, bring your deepest needs to the Friend who cares and who will carry you through all the storms of this life, and into his very presence.
* What do the next few days hold for you? Will there be encounters with difficult people? Will there be sorrow or solitude? Ask God to make you mindful of his presence and sensitive to the leading of his Spirit so that you can navigate these things according to his will.
* Finally, make time for worship. Ask God to clear your mind of extraneous concerns so that you can truly find joy in praising him for who he is and what he's done for you.

RESOURCES

RESOURCE NO. 1

Traditional Prayers & Readings

The Book of Common Prayer (BCP) is a scripture-based book of worship that originated in the heart of the English Reformation (1549). Its authors drew extensively from medieval and ancient Christian liturgical[1] materials, translating them from Latin into English, and seeking at the same time to curtail and correct anything from those earlier periods that was not in alignment with the teaching of the Bible. Over the next century, adjustments were made to the original work to try to bring balance to the theological extremes in the English Church, resulting in the edition of 1662, which current editions continue to closely reflect. The BCP still supports the devotional lives of Anglican believers around the world, and has strongly influenced the worship resources of many other Christian denominations.

In addition to providing detailed orders of service for numerous circumstances and life events, the BCP also includes prayers and readings suited to each Sunday in the Christian calendar. Used in Christian worship for centuries, this "lectionary" pattern of reading and praying with scripture is a deeply thoughtful one that invites us to reflect upon the relationship between the texts that have been set together for a given day.

Included below are the prayers and scripture readings in the BCP assigned for the four Sundays in Advent, as well as for the last Sunday before Advent, which acts as an introduction to the season. They appear in the old English language of the BCP, which is similar to the King James Version of the Bible.

In case liturgical terms such as "Collect," "Introit," and "Gradual"

---

[1] *"Liturgical worship" is characterised by a formal order of service with prayers, scripture readings, responsories, psalms and hymns, all assembled and arranged to complement the Church calendar.*

are new to you (you'll find these designations used in the BCP excerpts below), let me offer a few quick explanations. The "Collect" is a prayer intended to gather together the prayers of the people into a "common" or unified congregational prayer. The Introit, Gradual, and Alleluia are typically sung or chanted excerpts from scripture (usually from the Psalms), which are woven between the other readings like contemplative prayers. The "Gloria Patri" is a doxology added to the end of the Introit throughout most of the Christian year. During the more solemn season of Advent, this is omitted (as are other forms and placements for the Gloria) so that it might have all the more impact when it is exclaimed, as it was by the angels, on Christmas Day.

THE SUNDAY NEXT BEFORE ADVENT

The Collect

Stir up, we beseech thee, O Lord, the wills of thy faithful people; that they, plenteously bringing forth the fruit of good works, may of thee be plenteously rewarded; through Jesus Christ our Lord, who liveth and reigneth with thee and the Holy Spirit, one God, world without end. *Amen.*

Introit: Psalm 85:1-7

ANITPHON: *O LORD, show thy mercy upon us, /*
and grant us thy salvation.
LORD, thou art become gracious unto thy land: /
thou hast restored the fortunes of Jacob.
Thou hast forgiven the offence of thy people, /
and covered all their sins.
Thou hast taken away all thy displeasure, /
and turned thyself from thy wrathful indignation.
Turn us then, O God our Saviour, /
and let thine anger cease from us.
Wilt thou be displeased at us for ever? /
and wilt thou stretch out thy wrath from one generation to another?

Wilt thou not turn again, and quicken us, /
that thy people may rejoice in thee?
REPEAT: *O LORD, show thy mercy upon us, /*
and grant us thy salvation.

GLORIA PATRI: *Glory be to the Father, and to the Son,*
and to the Holy Ghost /
As it was in the beginning, is now, and ever shall be,
world without end. Amen.

The Lesson (for the Epistle): Jeremiah 23:5-8

Behold, the days come, saith the LORD, that I will raise unto David a righteous Branch, and a King shall reign and prosper, and shall execute judgement and justice in the earth. In his days Judah shall be saved, and Israel shall dwell safely: and this is his name whereby he shall be called, *the LORD our Righteousness*. Therefore behold, the days come, saith the LORD, that they shall no more say, The LORD liveth, which brought up the children of Israel out of the land of Egypt; but, The LORD liveth, which brought up, and which led the seed of the house of Israel out of the north-country, and from all countries whither I had driven them; and they shall dwell in their own land.

Gradual: Psalm 85:8-13

I will hearken what the LORD God will say: /
for he shall speak peace unto his people and to his saints, and unto them that turn their heart to him.
Surely his salvation is nigh them that fear him, /
that glory may dwell in our land.
Mercy and truth are met together: /
righteousness and peace have kissed each other.
Truth springeth out of the earth; /
and righteousness hath looked down from heaven.
Yea, the LORD shall give what is good; /

and our land shall yield her increase.
Alleluia, alleluia. Righteousness shall go before him, /
and shall direct his going in the way. Alleluia.

The Gospel: John 1:35-45

Note: Some older versions of the BCP have John 6:5-14 as the Gospel reading for this day.

John the Baptist stood, with two of his disciples; and looking upon Jesus as he walked, he saith, Behold the Lamb of God! And the two disciples heard him speak, and they followed Jesus. Then Jesus turned, and saw them following, and saith unto them, What seek ye? They said unto him, Rabbi (which is, being interpreted, Master), where dwellest thou? He saith unto them, Come and see. They came and saw where he dwelt, and abode with him that day, for it was about the tenth hour. One of the two which heard John speak, and followed him, was Andrew, Simon Peter's brother. He first findeth his own brother, Simon, and saith unto him, We have found the Messiah (which is, being interpreted, the Christ). And he brought him to Jesus. And when Jesus beheld him, he said, Thou art Simon the son of John: thou shalt be called Cephas (which is, by interpretation, A stone). The day following, Jesus would go forth into Galilee, and findeth Philip, and saith unto him, Follow me. Now Philip was of Bethsaida, the city of Andrew and Peter. Philip findeth Nathanael, and saith unto him, We have found him of whom Moses in the law, and the prophets, did write, Jesus of Nazareth, the son of Joseph.

THE FIRST SUNDAY IN ADVENT

The Collect

Note: This Collect is repeated every day during the season of Advent until Christmas Eve.

Almighty God, give us grace that we may cast away the works of darkness, and put upon us the armour of light, now in the time of this mortal life, in which thy Son Jesus Christ came to visit us in great humility; that in the last day, when he shall come again in his glorious Majesty, to judge both the quick and the dead, we may rise to the life immortal; through him who liveth and reigneth with thee and the Holy Spirit, now and ever. *Amen.*

Introit: Psalm 25:1-7

Unto thee, O LORD, will I lift up my soul; /
my God, I have put my trust in thee.
O let me not be confounded, /
neither let mine enemies triumph over me.
For all they that hope in thee shall not be ashamed; /
but such as transgress without a cause shall be put to confusion.
Show me thy ways, O LORD, /
and teach me thy paths.
Lead me forth in thy truth, and teach me: /
for thou art the God of my salvation;
in thee is my hope all the day long.
Call to remembrance, O LORD, thy tender mercies, /
and thy loving-kindnesses, which have been ever of old.
O remember not the sins and offences of my youth; /
but according to thy mercy think thou upon me, O LORD, for thy goodness.

REPEAT: *Unto thee, O LORD, will I lift up my soul; /*
my God, I have put my trust in thee.

NO GLORIA PATRI.

The Epistle: Romans 13:8-14

Owe no man anything, but to love one another: for he that

loveth his neighbour hath fulfilled the law. For this, Thou shalt not commit adultery, Thou shalt not kill, Thou shalt not steal, Thou shalt not bear false witness, Thou shalt not covet; and if there be any other commandment, it is briefly comprehended in this saying, namely, Thou shalt love thy neighbour as thyself. Love worketh no ill to his neighbour; therefore love is the fulfilling of the law. And that, knowing the time, that now it is high time to awake out of sleep: for now is our salvation nearer than when we believed. The night is far spent, the day is at hand; let us therefore cast off the works of darkness, and let us put on the armour of light. Let us walk honestly as in the day; not in rioting and drunkenness, not in chambering and wantonness, not in strife and envying. But put ye on the Lord Jesus Christ, and make not provision for the flesh, to fulfil the lusts thereof.

Gradual & Alleluia: Psalm 85:4-7

Turn us, O God our Saviour, /
 and let thine anger cease from us.
Wilt thou be displeased at us forever? /
 and wilt thou stretch out thy wrath from one generation to another?
Wilt thou not turn again and quicken us, /
 that thy people may rejoice in thee?
Alleluia, alleluia. O LORD, show thy mercy upon us, /
 and grant us thy salvation. Alleluia.

The Gospel: Matthew 21:1-13

When they drew nigh unto Jerusalem, and were come to Bethphage, unto the mount of Olives, then sent Jesus two disciples, saying unto them, Go into the village over against you, and straightway ye shall find an ass tied, and a colt with her: loose them, and bring them unto me. And if any man say aught unto you, ye shall say, The Lord hath need of them; and straightway he will send them. All this was done, that it might be fulfilled which was spoken by the Prophet, saying,

Tell ye the daughter of Zion,
Behold, thy King cometh unto thee,
Meek, and sitting upon an ass,
And a colt the foal of an ass.

And the disciples went, and did as Jesus commanded them; and brought the ass, and the colt, and put on them their clothes, and they set him thereon. And a very great multitude spread their garments in the way; others cut down branches from the trees, and strawed them in the way. And the multitudes that went before, and that followed, cried, saying, Hosanna to the Son of David; Blessed is he that cometh in the Name of the Lord; Hosanna in the highest. And when he was come into Jerusalem all the city was moved, saying, Who is this? And the multitude said, This is Jesus the Prophet of Nazareth of Galilee. And Jesus went into the temple of God, and cast out all them that sold and bought in the temple; and overthrew the tables of the moneychangers, and the seats of them that sold doves; and said unto them, It is written, My house shall be called the house of prayer; but ye have made it a den of thieves.

THE SECOND SUNDAY IN ADVENT

The Collect

Blessed Lord, who hast caused all holy Scriptures to be written for our learning: Grant that we may in such wise hear them, read, mark, learn, and inwardly digest them, that by patience and comfort of thy holy Word, we may embrace and ever hold fast the blessed hope of everlasting life, which thou hast given us in our Saviour Jesus Christ. *Amen.*

Introit: Psalm 80:1-7

Hear, O thou Shepherd of Israel, thou that leadest
Joseph like a flock; /
show thyself also, thou that sittest upon the
cherubim.
Before Ephraim, Benjamin, and Manasseh, /
stir up thy strength, and come and help us.
Turn us again, O God; /
show the light of thy countenance,
and we shall be whole.
O LORD God of hosts, /
how long wilt thou be angry
with thy people that prayeth?
Thou hast fed them with the bread of tears, /
and hast given them plenteousness
of tears to drink.
Thou makest us a very strife unto our neighbours, /
and our enemies laugh us to scorn.
Turn us again, O God of hosts; /
show the light of thy countenance,
and we shall be whole.
REPEAT: *Hear, O thou Shepherd of Israel, thou that leadest*
Joseph like a flock; /
show thyself also, thou that sittest upon the cherubim.
NO GLORIA PATRI.

The Epistle: Romans 15:4-13

Whatsoever things were written aforetime were written for our learning; that we through patience and comfort of the Scriptures might have hope. Now the God of patience and consolation grant you to be like-minded one towards another, according to Christ Jesus: that ye may with one mind and one mouth glorify God, even the Father of our Lord Jesus Christ. Wherefore receive ye one another, as Christ also received us, to the glory of God. Now I say, that Jesus Christ was a minister of the circumcision for the truth of God, to confirm the promises made unto the fathers; and that the Gentiles might glorify God for his mercy; as it is written,

For this cause I will give praise to thee among the Gentiles,
And sing unto thy Name.

And again he saith,

Rejoice, ye Gentiles, with his people.

And again,

Praise the Lord, all ye Gentiles, and laud him, all ye people.

And again, Isaiah saith,

There shall be a root of Jesse,
And he that shall rise to reign over the Gentiles,
In him shall the Gentiles hope.

Now the God of hope fill you with all joy and peace in believing, that ye may abound in hope, in the power of the Holy Spirit.

Gradual & Alleluia: Psalm 50:1-6

The LORD, even the most mighty God, hath spoken, /
  and called the world, from the rising up
  of the sun unto the going down thereof.
Out of Zion, the perfection of beauty, /
  God hath shined forth.
Our God cometh, and keepeth not silence; /
  there goeth before him a consuming fire,
  and a mighty tempest is stirred up
  round about him.
He calleth to the heavens from above, /

and to the earth, that he may judge his people:
"Gather my saints together unto me: /
those that have made a covenant with me
with sacrifice."
Alleluia, alleluia.
And the heavens declare his righteousness; /
for God is judge himself. Alleluia.

The Gospel: Luke 21:25-33

Jesus said unto his disciples, There shall be signs in the sun, and in the moon, and in the stars; and upon the earth distress of nations, with perplexity, the sea and the waves roaring; men's hearts failing them for fear, and for looking after those things which are coming on the earth: for the powers of heaven shall be shaken. And then shall they see the Son of Man coming in a cloud with power and great glory. And when these things begin to come to pass, then look up, and lift up your heads; for your redemption draweth nigh. And he spake to them a parable; Behold the fig-tree, and all the trees; when they now shoot forth, ye see and know of your own selves that summer is now nigh at hand. So likewise ye, when ye see these things come to pass, know ye that the kingdom of God is nigh at hand. Verily I say unto you, This generation shall not pass away, till all be fulfilled: heaven and earth shall pass away; but my words shall not pass away.

THE THIRD SUNDAY IN ADVENT

The Collect

O Lord Jesus Christ, who at thy first coming didst send thy messenger to prepare thy way before thee: Grant that the ministers and stewards of thy mysteries may likewise so prepare and make ready thy way, by turning the hearts of the disobedient to the wisdom of the just, that at thy second coming to judge the world we may be found an acceptable people in thy sight; who livest and reignest with the Father and the Holy Spirit, ever one God, world without end. *Amen.*

Introit: Psalm 33:1-6

Rejoice in the LORD, O ye righteous; /
for it becometh well the just to be thankful.
Praise the LORD with harp: /
sing praises unto him with the lute,
and instrument of ten strings.
Sing unto the LORD a new song: /
sing praises lustily with a good courage.
For the word of the LORD is true, /
and all his works are faithful.
He loveth righteousness and judgement: /
the earth is full of the goodness of the LORD.
By the word of the LORD were the heavens made, /
and all the hosts of them by the breath
of his mouth.
REPEAT: Rejoice in the LORD, O ye righteous; /
for it becometh well the just to be thankful.
NO GLORIA PATRI.

The Epistle: 1 Corinthians 4:1-5

Let a man so account of us, as of the ministers of Christ, and stewards of the mysteries of God. Moreover, it is required in stewards, that a man be found faithful. But with me it is a very small thing that I should be judged of you, or of man's judgement: yea, I judge not mine own self. I know nothing against myself, yet am I not hereby justified; but he that judgeth me is the Lord. Therefore judge nothing before the time, until the Lord come, who both will bring to light the hidden things of darkness, and will make manifest the counsels of the hearts; and then shall every man have praise of God.

Gradual & Alleluia: Psalm 80:1-3

Hear, O thou Shepherd of Israel,
thou that leadest Joseph like a flock; /
show thyself also, thou that sittest
upon the cherubim.
Before Ephraim, Benjamin, and Manasseh, /
stir up thy strength, and come and help us.
Alleluia, alleluia. Turn us again, O God; /
show the light of thy countenance,
and we shall be whole. Alleluia.

The Gospel: Matthew 11:2-10

Now when John had heard in the prison the works of Christ, he sent two of his disciples, and said unto him, Art thou he that should come, or do we look for another? Jesus answered and said unto them, Go and show John again those things which ye do hear and see: the blind receive their sight, and the lame walk, the lepers are cleansed, and the deaf hear, the dead are raised up, and the poor have the Gospel preached to them. And blessed is he whosoever shall not be offended in me. And as they departed, Jesus began to say unto the multitudes concerning John, What went ye out into the wilderness to see? A reed shaken with the wind? But what went ye out for to see? A man clothed in soft raiment? Behold, they that wear soft clothing are in kings' houses. But what went ye out for to see? A prophet? Yea, I say unto you, and more than a prophet. For this is he of whom it is written,

Behold, I send my messenger before thy face,
Which shall prepare thy way before thee.

THE FOURTH SUNDAY IN ADVENT

The Collect

Raise up, we beseech thee, O Lord, thy power, and come among us, and with great might succour us; that whereas, through our sins and wickedness, we are sore let and hindered in running the race that is set before us, thy bountiful grace and mercy may speedily help and deliver us; who with the Father and the Holy Spirit livest and reignest, one God, world without end. *Amen.*

Introit: Psalm 19:1-6

The heavens declare the glory of God; /
    and the firmament showeth his handy-work.
One day telleth another; /
    and one night certifieth another.
There is neither speech nor language; /
    their voice cannot be heard;
Yet their sound is gone out into all lands; /
    and their words into the ends of the world.
In them hath he set a tabernacle for the sun; /
    which cometh forth as a bridegroom out of
    his chamber, and rejoiceth as a giant to run his
    course.
It goeth forth from the uttermost part of the heaven,
    and runneth about unto the end of it again; /
    and there is nothing hid from the heat thereof.
REPEAT: *In them hath he set a tabernacle for the sun; /*
    which cometh forth as a bridegroom out of
    his chamber, and rejoiceth as a giant to run his course.
NO GLORIA PATRI.

The Epistle: Philippians 4:4-7

Rejoice in the Lord alway, and again I say, Rejoice. Let your moderation be known unto all men. The Lord is at hand. In nothing be anxious: but in everything, by prayer and supplication with thanksgiving, let your requests be made known unto God. And the peace of God, which passeth all understanding, shall keep your hearts and minds through Christ Jesus.

Gradual & Alleluia: Psalm 145:18-22

The LORD is righteous in all his ways, /
  and holy in all his works.
The LORD is nigh unto all them that call upon him, /
  yea, all such as call upon him faithfully.
He will fulfil the desire of them that fear him: /
  and he also will hear their cry,
  and will help them.
The LORD preserveth all them that love him; /
  but scattereth abroad all the ungodly.
Alleluia, alleluia.
  My mouth shall speak the praise of the LORD: /
  and let all flesh give thanks unto his holy Name
  for ever and ever. Alleluia.

The Gospel: John 1:19-29

This is the witness of John, when the Jews sent Priests and Levites from Jerusalem to ask him, Who art thou? And he confessed, and denied not; and he confessed, I am not the Christ. And they asked him, What then? Art thou Elijah? And he said, I am not. Art thou the Prophet? And he answered, No. Then said they unto him, Who art thou? that we may give an answer to them that sent us. What sayest thou of thyself? He said, I am the voice of one crying in the wilderness, Make straight the way of the Lord, as said the prophet Isaiah. And they which were sent were of the Pharisees. And they asked him, and said unto him, Why baptisest thou then, if thou be not the Christ, nor Elijah, nor the Prophet? John answered them, saying, I baptise with water, but there standeth one among you, whom ye know not: he it is who cometh after me, whose shoe's latchet I am not worthy to unloose. These things were done in Bethany beyond Jordan, where John was baptising. The next day John seeth Jesus coming unto him, and saith, Behold the Lamb of God, which taketh away the sin of the world.

RESOURCE NO. 2

The Litany

The Litany is a responsive intercessory prayer that has its origin in the fourth century. It is the oldest part of the Book of Common Prayer[2] *(BCP), except for the scriptures themselves.*

Pre-Reformation versions of the Litany often included a lengthy section appealing to the intercession of the saints ("Mother of God, pray for us; Holy Apostles, pray for us..."). The BCP version corrects this, recognising the Lord Jesus as the only mediator between God and humanity—but it does have one notable drawback. It tends to conflate matters of church and state. This is due to the fact that the head of the Church of England—from which the BCP comes to us—is the King or Queen of that country. A more Protestant rendering of the Litany should retain only those prayers for the state which are consistent with New Testament teaching, and clearly appeal to Christ *as the head of the Church universal, with the many leaders of many denominations serving under that headship. With this in view, I've omitted a brief section of petitions for the British monarchy from the version of the Litany included below. This aside, the Litany is a wonderful prayer and a most thorough intercession, which assists us in seeking God's involvement and aid in every aspect of our lives, communities and churches.*

While many liturgical churches once recommended that the Litany be prayed three times weekly, this has not been the fashion for several generations, due largely to its somber and penitential tone. It is still traditional practice, however, for the Litany to be prayed or sung, often in procession, on the first Sundays of Lent and Advent.

LEADER: O God the Father,
Creator of heaven and earth:
have mercy upon us.

[2] *See the first paragraph of the introductory notes on page 99 for more information about the Book of Common Prayer.*

RESPONSE: *O God the Father, Creator of heaven and earth:*
have mercy upon us.

LEADER: O God the Son, Redeemer of the world:
have mercy upon us.
RESPONSE: *O God the Son, Redeemer of the world:*
have mercy upon us.

LEADER: O God the Holy Ghost,
Sanctifier of the faithful:
have mercy upon us.
RESPONSE: *O God the Holy Ghost,*
Sanctifier of the faithful:
have mercy upon us.

LEADER: O holy, blessed, and glorious Trinity,
three Persons and one God:
have mercy upon us.
RESPONSE: *O holy, blessed, and glorious Trinity,*
three Persons and one God:
have mercy upon us.

LEADER: Remember not, Lord, our offences,
nor the offences of our forefathers;
spare us, good Lord, spare thy people,
whom thou hast redeemed
with thy most precious blood.
RESPONSE: *Spare us, good Lord.*

LEADER: From all evil and mischief;
from sin,
from the crafts and assaults of the devil;
from thy wrath,
and from everlasting condemnation,
RESPONSE: *Good Lord, deliver us.*

LEADER: From all blindness of heart;
from pride, vainglory, and hypocrisy;
from envy, hatred, and malice,
and all uncharitableness,
RESPONSE: *Good Lord, deliver us.*

LEADER: From all uncleanness in thought,
word, and deed;
and from all the deceits of the world,
the flesh, and the devil,
RESPONSE: *Good Lord, deliver us.*

LEADER: From lightning and tempest;
from earthquake, fire, and flood;
from plague, pestilence, and famine;
from battle and murder,
and from sudden death,
RESPONSE: *Good Lord, deliver us.*

LEADER: From all sedition, conspiracy, and rebellion;
from all false doctrine, heresy, and schism;
from hardness of heart, and contempt
of thy Word and Commandment,
RESPONSE: *Good Lord, deliver us.*

LEADER: By the mystery of thy holy Incarnation;
by thy holy Nativity;
by thy Baptism, Fasting, and Temptation,
RESPONSE: *Good Lord, deliver us.*

LEADER: By thine Agony and bloody Sweat;
by thy Cross and Passion;
by thy precious Death and Burial,
RESPONSE: *Good Lord, deliver us.*

LEADER: By thy glorious Resurrection and Ascension;
by thy sending of the Holy Spirit;
by thy heavenly Intercession;
and by thy Coming again in glory,
RESPONSE: *Good Lord, deliver us.*

LEADER: In all times of tribulation;
in all times of prosperity;
in the hour of death,
and in the day of judgement,
RESPONSE: *Good Lord, deliver us.*

LEADER: We sinners do beseech thee to hear us,
O Lord God;
And that it may please thee
to rule and govern thy holy Church universal
in the right way,
RESPONSE: *We beseech thee, good Lord.*

(INTERCESSIONS FOR THE QUEEN AS THE HEAD OF THE CHURCH OF ENGLAND AND FOR THE ROYAL FAMILY HAVE BEEN OMITTED.)

LEADER: To give to all Bishops, Priests, and Deacons,
true knowledge and understanding
of thy Word;
and that both by their preaching and living
they may set it forth and show it accordingly,
RESPONSE: *We beseech thee, good Lord.*

LEADER: To send forth labourers into thy harvest;
to prosper their work by thy Holy Spirit;
to make thy saving health known
unto all nations; and to hasten thy kingdom,
RESPONSE: *We beseech thee, good Lord.*

LEADER: To bless the people of our Country,
[and the Commonwealth,]
and to endue those set in authority
with grace, wisdom, and understanding,
RESPONSE: *We beseech thee, good Lord.*

LEADER: To bless and guide the Judges
and Magistrates, giving them grace
to execute justice, and to maintain truth,
RESPONSE: *We beseech thee, good Lord.*

LEADER: To bless and keep [the Queen's] forces
by sea, and land, and air, and to shield them
in all dangers and adversities,
RESPONSE: *We beseech thee, good Lord.*

LEADER: To give to all nations
unity, peace, and concord,
that they may serve thee without fear,
RESPONSE: *We beseech thee, good Lord.*

LEADER: To bless and protect all who serve mankind
by their labour and learning,
RESPONSE: *We beseech thee, good Lord.*

LEADER: To preserve all that travel,
all women labouring of child,
all sick persons and young children;
and to show thy pity upon
all prisoners and captives,
RESPONSE: *We beseech thee, good Lord.*

LEADER: To defend and provide
for all widows and orphans,
and all who are desolate and oppressed,
RESPONSE: *We beseech thee, good Lord.*

LEADER: To bless and keep all thy people,
RESPONSE: *We beseech thee, good Lord.*

LEADER: To give to all thy people increase of grace,
to hear meekly thy Word,
and to receive it with pure affection,
and to bring forth the fruit of the Spirit,
RESPONSE: *We beseech thee, good Lord.*

LEADER: To bring into the way of truth
all who have erred and are deceived,
RESPONSE: *We beseech thee, good Lord.*

LEADER: To strengthen such as do stand;
to encourage the faint-hearted;
to raise up those who fall;
and finally to beat down Satan
under our feet,
RESPONSE: *We beseech thee, good Lord.*

LEADER: To succour, help, and comfort
all that are in danger, necessity,
and tribulation,
RESPONSE: *We beseech thee, good Lord.*

LEADER: To have mercy upon all men,
RESPONSE: *We beseech thee, good Lord.*

LEADER: To give and preserve to our use
the kindly fruits of the earth,
so that in due time we may enjoy them,
RESPONSE: *We beseech thee, good Lord.*

LEADER: To forgive our enemies, persecutors,
and slanderers, and to turn their hearts,
RESPONSE: *We beseech thee, good Lord.*

LEADER: To give us true repentance;
to forgive us all our sins, negligences,
and ignorances;
and to endue us with the grace
of thy Holy Spirit, to amend our lives
according to thy holy Word,
RESPONSE: *We beseech thee, good Lord.*

LEADER: Son of God, we beseech thee to hear us.
RESPONSE: *Son of God, we beseech thee to hear us.*

LEADER: O Lamb of God,
that takest away the sin of the world;
RESPONSE: *Have mercy upon us.*

LEADER: O Lamb of God,
that takest away the sin of the world;
RESPONSE: *Grant us thy peace.*

LEADER: O Christ hear us.
RESPONSE: *O Christ hear us.*

LEADER: Lord, have mercy upon us.
RESPONSE: *Christ, have mercy upon us.*
LEADER: Lord, have mercy upon us.

LEADER: Our Father who art in heaven,
Hallowed be thy Name,
Thy kingdom come,
Thy will be done, on earth as it is in heaven.
Give us this day our daily bread;
And forgive us our trespasses,
As we forgive them that trespass against us;

And lead us not into temptation,
But deliver us from evil.
RESPONSE: *Amen.*

LEADER: Almighty God,
who hast given us grace at this time
with one accord to make
our common supplications unto thee;
and dost promise that when two or three
are gathered together in thy Name
thou wilt grant their requests:
Fulfil now, O Lord, the desires and petitions
of thy servants, as may be most expedient
for them; granting us in this world
knowledge of thy truth,
and in the world to come life everlasting.
RESPONSE: *Amen.*

LEADER: The grace of our Lord Jesus Christ,
and the love of God, and the fellowship
of the Holy Ghost, be with us all evermore.
RESPONSE: *Amen.*

RESOURCE NO. 3

Advent Prose (Rorate Caeli)

This beautiful liturgical responsory dates from fourth century Spain and is sometimes attributed to a Christian poet named Aurelius Clemens Prudentius—although this attribution is uncertain. What we do know is that "Rorate Cæli" was written as a responsive chant, and has been used in Christian worship during the season of Advent for centuries. It was translated from Latin into English in the 17th century, and in this form it is usually referred to simply as "Advent Prose."

The text of this piece is a reworking of several passages from the Old Testament book of Isaiah that give voice to the repentance of God's people and their longing for his promised salvation to appear. The title "Rorate Cæli" refers to the opening line in Latin, which translates as "Drop down, ye heavens" (ISAIAH 45:8 KJV).

There are several musical settings which have been written for both the Latin and the English versions, though Rorate Cæli is most commonly sung in a pared down "plainchant" style which is in keeping with the quiet, reflective spirit of the season. The italicized "antiphon" is usually repeated by all (like a refrain), with the verses being sung by a single voice.

ANTIPHON: *Drop down, ye heavens, from above;*
And let the skies pour down righteousness.

Be not wroth very sore, O Lord,
neither remember iniquity forever:
Thy holy city is a wilderness,
Zion is a wilderness, Jerusalem a desolation:
Our holy and our beautiful house,

where our fathers praised thee.

REPEAT: *Drop down, ye heavens, from above;*
And let the skies pour down righteousness.

We have sinned, and are as an unclean thing,
and we all do fade as a leaf:
And our iniquities, like the wind, have taken us away:
Thou hast hid thy face from us:
And hast consumed us, because of our iniquities.

REPEAT: *Drop down, ye heavens, from above;*
And let the skies pour down righteousness.

Behold, O Lord, the affliction of thy people,
and send forth him whom thou wilt send;
Send forth the Lamb, the ruler of the earth,
from Petra of the desert to the mount
of the daughter of Zion:
That he may take away the yoke of our captivity.

REPEAT: *Drop down, ye heavens, from above;*
And let the skies pour down righteousness.

Ye are my witnesses, saith the Lord,
and my servant whom I have chosen;
That ye may know me and believe me:
I, even I, am the Lord, and beside me
there is no Saviour:
And there is none that can deliver out of my hand.

REPEAT: *Drop down, ye heavens, from above;*
And let the skies pour down righteousness.

Comfort ye, comfort ye my people;
My salvation shall not tarry:
Why wilt thou waste away in sadness?

Why hath sorrow seized thee?
Fear not, for I will save thee:
For I am the Lord thy God,
the Holy One of Israel, thy Redeemer.

REPEAT: *Drop down, ye heavens, from above;*
And let the skies pour down righteousness.

RESOURCE NO. 4

Hymns & Carols

There is an unfortunate tendency in modern churches to sing Christmas hymns and carols throughout the season of Advent. This is a bit like eating our favourite food at every meal of every day—until we have all but forgotten that there are other wonderful and nutritious foods we should include in our diet in order to be balanced and healthy. Though many of the traditional hymns and carols of Advent have fallen out of popular use, they have not disappeared. We simply need to make room for them again.

An important way to help preserve the integrity of Advent (and Christmas as well), is to save Christmas music for Christmas itself, and to discover and enjoy the wonderful trove of lesser-known Advent hymns in the four weeks prior. The key difference between the two is that the music of Advent focuses upon our longing for Christ's coming or upon the events that led to the incarnation, rather than on the joy of Christ's nativity.

Included below is a selection of traditional Advent music (arranged in alphabetical order by title). I've offered a brief note of introduction to each, as well as musical notes for worship leaders where possible. Carols have a tendency to be more "festive," whereas the hymns are more "worshipful," so I've only included here those carols which (in my opinion) are sufficiently substantial to be devotionally useful.

COME, THOU LONG EXPECTED JESUS

Penned by prolific eighteenth century Protestant hymn writer Charles Wesley, this is one of the few Advent hymns that is still widely used.

METRE: 8.7.8.7 | SUGGESTED TUNES: HYFRYDOL, STUTTGART

Come, thou long expected Jesus,
Born to set thy people free,

From our fears and sins release us,
Let us find our rest in thee:
Israel's strength and consolation,
Hope of all the earth thou art,
Dear desire of every nation,
Joy of every longing heart.

Born thy people to deliver,
Born a child and yet a king,
Born to reign in us forever,
Now thy gracious kingdom bring:
By thy own eternal Spirit
Rule in all our hearts alone,
By thy all-sufficient merit
Raise us to thy glorious throne.

COME, THOU REDEEMER OF THE EARTH (VENI REDEMPTOR GENTIUM)

This ancient hymn is generally attributed to Ambrose of Milan in the 4th century. It was translated from Latin to English in the 1800s by John Mason Neale.

METRE: 8.8.8.8 | SUGGESTED TUNE: PUER NOBIS NASCITUR

Come, thou Redeemer of the earth,
And manifest thy virgin birth:
Let every age adoring fall;
Such birth befits the God of all.

Begotten of no human will,
But of the Spirit, thou art still
The Word of God in flesh arrayed,
The promised fruit to men displayed.

The virgin womb that burden gained
With virgin honour all unstained;

The banners there of virtue glow;
God in his temple dwells below.

Forth from his chamber goeth he,
That royal home of purity,
A giant in two-fold substance one,
Rejoicing now his course to run.

From God the Father he proceeds,
To God the Father back he speeds;
His course he runs to death and hell,
Returning on God's throne to dwell.

O equal to the Father, thou!
Gird on thy fleshly mantle now;
The weakness of our mortal state
With deathless might invigorate!

Thy cradle here shall glitter bright
And darkness breathe a newer light,
Where endless faith shall shine serene,
And twilight never intervene.

CREATOR OF THE STARS OF NIGHT (CONDITOR ALME SIDERUM)

This is another ancient Latin hymn that dates back to the early Middle Ages; it was also translated into English by John Mason Neale in the 1800s.

METRE: 8.8.8.8 | SUGGESTED TUNES: ST. AMBROSE, ANGEL'S SONG, PUER NOBIS NASCITUR

Creator of the stars of night,
Thy people's everlasting light,
Jesu, Redeemer, save us all,
And hear thy servants when they call.

Thou, grieving that the ancient curse

Should doom to death a universe,
Hast found the medicine, full of grace,
To save and heal a ruined race.

Thou cam'st, the Bridegroom of the bride,
As drew the world to evening-tide;
Proceeding from a virgin shrine,
The spotless Victim all divine.

At whose dread name, majestic now,
All knees must bend, all hearts must bow;
And things celestial, thee shall own,
And things terrestrial, lord alone.

O thou whose coming is with dread
To judge and doom the quick and dead,
Preserve us, while we dwell below,
From every insult of the foe.

To God the Father, God the Son,
And God the Spirit, Three in One,
Laud, honour, might, and glory be
From age to age eternally.

GABRIEL'S MESSAGE

First, there was the scriptural account of the angelic announcement to Mary in Luke's gospel. Then, there came a Latin carol based on this text in the 13th century ("Angelus Ad Virginem" meaning "The angel came to the virgin"). This then inspired a Basque folk carol which finally came to be rendered in its well-known English form by Sabine Baring-Gould (1834-1924). During the season of Advent, the fourth verse of the carol should be omitted.

METRE: 10.10.12.10 | SUGGESTED TUNE: GABRIEL'S MESSAGE

The angel Gabriel from heaven came,
His wings as drifted snow, his eyes as flame.

"All hail," said he, "thou lowly maiden Mary,
Most highly favoured lady." Gloria!

"For know a blessed mother thou shalt be,
All generations laud and honour thee,
Thy son shall be Emmanuel, by seers foretold,
Most highly favoured lady." Gloria!

Then gentle Mary meekly bowed her head.
"To me be as it pleaseth God," she said,
"My soul shall laud and magnify his holy name."
Most highly favoured lady. Gloria!

Of her, Emmanuel, the Christ was born,
In Bethlehem, on Christmas morn,
And Christian folk throughout the world will ever say:
"Most highly favoured lady." Gloria!

HARK! A HERALD VOICE IS CALLING (EN CLARA VOX REDARGUIT)

Based on a Latin hymn of the 6th century, this was translated into English by Rev. Edward Caswall in the 19th century.

METRE: 8.7.8.7 | SUGGESTED TUNE: MERTON

Hark! A herald voice is calling:
"Christ is nigh," it seems to say;
"Cast away the dreams of darkness,
O ye children of the day!"

Startled at the solemn warning,
Let the earth-bound soul arise;
Christ, her sun, all sloth dispelling,
Shines upon the morning skies.

Lo! The Lamb, so long expected,
Comes with pardon down from heaven;
Let us haste, with tears of sorrow,

One and all to be forgiven;

So when next he comes with glory,
Wrapping all the earth in fear,
May he then as our defender
Of the clouds of heaven appear.

Honour, glory, virtue, merit,
To the Father and the Son,
With the co-eternal Spirit,
While unending ages run.

JESUS CAME, THE HEAVENS ADORING

This hymn was written in the 19th century by Godfrey Thring, an Anglican clergyman who is best remembered for the verses he contributed to the hymn "Crown Him With Many Crowns."

METRE: 8.7.8.7.8.7 | SUGGESTED TUNES: PICARDY, LAUDA ANIMA, ST. THOMAS, HELMSLEY

Jesus came, the heavens adoring,
Came with peace from realms on high;
Jesus came for man's redemption,
Lowly came on earth to die;
Alleluia! Alleluia!
Came in deep humility.

Jesus comes again in mercy
When our hearts are bowed with care;
Jesus comes again in answer
To an earnest, heartfelt prayer;
Alleluia! Alleluia!
Comes to save us from despair.

Jesus comes to hearts rejoicing,
Bringing news of sins forgiven;
Jesus comes in sounds of gladness,
Leading souls redeemed to heaven.

Alleluia! Alleluia!
Now the gate of death is riven.

Jesus comes in joy and sorrow,
Shares alike our hopes and fears;
Jesus comes, whate'er befalls us,
Glads our hearts, and dries our tears;
Alleluia! Alleluia!
Cheering e'en our failing years.

Jesus comes on clouds triumphant
When the heavens shall pass away;
Jesus comes again in glory.
Let us, then, our homage pay,
Alleluia! Ever singing
Till the dawn of endless day.

JESUS CHRIST, THE APPLE TREE

An unusual 18th century carol, this text is inspired by Song of Solomon 2:3 ("Like an apple tree among the trees of the forest is my beloved among the young men"). It compares Jesus to an apple tree, entering into the spirit of longing which characterises the season of Advent.

SHEET MUSIC FOR ELIZABETH POSTON'S SETTING (SUGGESTED) CAN BE FOUND ONLINE

The Tree of Life my soul hath seen,
Laden with fruit and always green;
The trees of nature fruitless be,
Compared with Christ the Apple Tree.

His beauty doth all things excel,
By faith I know but ne'er can tell
The glory which I now can see,
In Jesus Christ the Apple Tree.

For happiness I long have sought,

And pleasure dearly I have bought;
I missed of all but now I see
'Tis found in Christ the Apple Tree.

I'm weary with my former toil -
Here I will sit and rest awhile,
Under the shadow I will be,
Of Jesus Christ the Apple Tree.

With great delight I'll make my stay,
There's none shall fright my soul away;
Among the sons of men I see
There's none like Christ the Apple Tree.

I'll sit and eat this fruit divine,
It cheers my heart like spirit'al wine;
And now this fruit is sweet to me,
That grows on Christ the Apple Tree.

This fruit doth make my soul to thrive,
It keeps my dying faith alive;
Which makes my soul in haste to be
With Jesus Christ the Apple Tree.

LO, HE COMES, WITH CLOUDS DESCENDING

Originally penned by prolific eighteenth century Protestant hymn writer Charles Wesley, the lyrics of this hymn have been subsequently altered numerous times for use in various denominations, with slightly different eschatological emphases.

METRE: 8.7.8.7.4.7 | SUGGESTED TUNE: HELMSLEY

Lo, he comes, with clouds descending,
Once for favoured sinners slain;
Thousand, thousand saints attending
Swell the triumph of his train:

Alleluia: Christ appears on earth again.

Every eye shall now behold him,
Robed in dreadful majesty;
Those who set at naught and sold him,
Pierced, and nailed him to the tree,
Deeply wailing: Shall the true Messiah see.

Those dear tokens of his passion
Still his dazzling body bears,
Cause of endless exultation
To his ransomed worshippers:
With what rapture: Gaze we on those glorious scars!

Now redemption, long expected,
See in solemn pomp appear:
All his saints, by men rejected,
Now shall meet him in the air:
Alleluia: See the day of God appear.

Yea, amen; let all adore thee,
High on thine eternal throne;
Saviour, take the power and glory;
Claim the kingdoms for thine own:
Alleluia! Thou shalt reign, and thou alone.

Yet with mingled hope and fearing,
Wait we still our Judge to see;
In the day of thine appearing.
Spotless, blameless may we be!
Ever watching: Teach us, Lord, to welcome thee.

O COME, DIVINE MESSIAH! (VENEZ DIVIN MESSIE)

Originally written in French by Abbot Simon J. Pellegrin (1663-1745), this hymn was translated into English in the 19th century by Frances Mary Lescher, who is more commonly remembered as Sister

Mary of St. Philip, a nun associated with a religious community in France called Notre Dame de Namur.

METRE: 7.8.7.6.8.8.8 | SUGGESTED TUNE: VENEZ, DIVIN MESSIE

O come, divine Messiah!
The world in silence waits the day
When hope shall sing its triumph,
And sadness flee away.

Dear Saviour haste; Come, come to earth,
Dispel the night and show your face,
And bid us hail the dawn of grace.

O come, divine Messiah!
The world in silence waits the day
When hope shall sing its triumph,
And sadness flee away.

O Christ, whom nations sigh for,
Whom priest and prophet long foretold,
Come break the captive fetters;
Redeem the long-lost fold.

Dear Saviour haste; Come, come to earth,
Dispel the night and show your face,
And bid us hail the dawn of grace.

O come, divine Messiah!
The world in silence waits the day
When hope shall sing its triumph,
And sadness flee away.

You come in peace and meekness,
And lowly will your cradle be;
All clothed in human weakness
Shall we your Godhead see.

Dear Saviour haste; Come, come to earth,
Dispel the night and show your face,

And bid us hail the dawn of grace.

O come, divine Messiah!
The world in silence waits the day
When hope shall sing its triumph,
And sadness flee away.

O COME, O COME EMMANUEL (VENI, VENI, EMMANUEL)

An ancient hymn of the Church, this was originally written in Latin in the early Middle Ages and translated into the familiar English version by John Mason Neale in 1851, with additional verses added by H.S. Coffin in 1916. (The original Latin hymn was inspired by the liturgical "O Antiphons," see page 149 for further details).

METRE: 8.8.8.8.8.8 | SUGGESTED TUNE: VENI EMMANUEL

O come, O come, Emmanuel,
And ransom captive Israel,
That mourns in lonely exile here,
Until the Son of God appear.
Rejoice! Rejoice! Emmanuel
Shall come to thee, O Israel.

O come, thou Rod of Jesse, free
Thine own from Satan's tyranny;
From depths of hell thy people save,
And give them victory o'er the grave.
Rejoice! Rejoice! Emmanuel
Shall come to thee, O Israel.

O come, thou Dayspring, from on high,
And cheer us by thy drawing nigh;
Disperse the gloomy clouds of night,
And death's dark shadows put to flight.
Rejoice! Rejoice! Emmanuel
Shall come to thee, O Israel.

O come, thou Key of David, come,
And open wide our heav'nly home;
Make safe the way that leads on high,
And close the path to misery.
Rejoice! Rejoice! Emmanuel
Shall come to thee, O Israel.

O come, Adonai, Lord of might,
Who to thy tribes on Sinai's height,
In ancient times didst give the law,
In cloud and majesty and awe.
Rejoice! Rejoice! Emmanuel
Shall come to thee, O Israel.

O come, thou Wisdom from on high,
And order all things, far and nigh;
To us the path of knowledge show,
And cause us in her ways to go.
Rejoice! Rejoice! Emmanuel
Shall come to thee, O Israel.

O come, Desire of nations, bind
All peoples in one heart and mind;
Bid envy, strife and quarrels cease;
Fill the whole world with heaven's peace.
Rejoice! Rejoice! Emmanuel
Shall come to thee, O Israel.

O HEAVENLY WORD, ETERNAL LIGHT (VERBUM SUPERNUM PRODIENS)

Originally dating to at least the 6th century, and sometimes attributed to Ambrose of Milan, this hymn was translated into English from Latin in the 19th century by John Mason Neale.

METRE: 8.8.8.8 | SUGGESTED TUNE: VERBUM SUPERNUM PRODIENS

O Heavenly Word, Eternal Light,

Begotten of the Father's might,
Who in these latter days art born
For succour to a world forlorn.

Our hearts enlighten from above,
And kindle with thine own true love,
That we, who hear thy call today,
May cast earth's vanities away.

And when as Judge thou drawest nigh,
The secrets of our hearts to try,
When sinners meet their awful doom,
And saints attain their heavenly home;

O let us not, for evil past,
Be driven from thy face at last,
But with the blessed evermore,
Behold thee, love thee, and adore.

To God the Father, God the Son,
And God the Spirit, Three in One,
Praise, honour, might and glory be,
From age to age eternally.

ON JORDAN'S BANK, THE BAPTIST'S CRY (JORDANIS ORAS PRÆVIA)

This hymn is especially appropriate for the third Sunday in Advent, as it focuses upon the role of John the Baptist as the forerunner of Christ. Originally in Latin, it was penned in the 18th century by Charles Coffin, and translated into English by John Chandler a century later.

METRE: 8.8.8.8 | SUGGESTED TUNE: WINCHESTER NEW

On Jordan's bank, the baptist's cry
Announces that the Lord is nigh;
Awake, and hearken, for he brings

Glad tidings of the King of kings!

Then cleansed be every breast from sin;
Make straight the way for God within;
Prepare we in our hearts a home
Where such a mighty guest may come.

For thou art our salvation, Lord,
Our refuge, and our great reward.
Without thy grace we waste away,
Like flowers that wither and decay.

To heal the sick, stretch out thine hand,
And bid the fallen sinner stand;
Shine forth, and let thy light restore
Earth's own true loveliness once more.

Stretch forth thine hand to heal our sore,
And make us rise, to fall no more;
Once more upon thy people shine,
And fill the world with love divine.

All praise, eternal Son, to thee
Whose advent sets thy people free,
Whom, with the Father, we adore,
And Holy Ghost, forevermore.

REJOICE, ALL YE BELIEVERS (ERMUNTERT EUCH, IHR FROMMEN)

A beautiful hymn canvassing all the themes of Advent, this was first introduced to an English audience in 1854 by Sarah Findlater's book of translations, "Hymns from the Land of Luther." It was originally written in German by Laurentius Laurenti (1660-1722).

METRE: 7.6.7.6 | SUGGESTED TUNE: LANCASHIRE

Rejoice, all ye believers,
And let your lights appear!

The evening is advancing,
And darker night is near.
The Bridegroom is arising,
And soon he draweth nigh.
Up, watch, and pray, and wrestle,
At midnight comes the cry!

The watchers on the mountain
Proclaim the Bridegroom near;
Go meet him as he cometh,
With hallelujahs clear.
The marriage feast is waiting,
The gates wide open stand!
Up, up, ye heirs of glory,
The Bridegroom is at hand!

Ye saints, who here in patience
Your cross and suff'rings bore,
Shall live and reign forever,
Where sorrow is no more.
Around the throne of glory
The Lamb ye shall behold,
In triumph cast before him
Your diadems of gold!

Our hope and expectation,
O Jesus now appear;
Arise, thou sun so longed for,
O'er this benighted sphere!
With hearts and hands uplifted,
We plead, O Lord, to see
The day of earth's redemption,
That brings us unto thee!

THE ADVENT OF OUR GOD (INSTANTIS ADVENTUM DEI)

Originally in Latin, this hymn was penned in the 18th century by Charles Coffin, and translated into English by John Chandler a century later. Several variations of this hymn exist, including versions by other translators.

METRE: 6.6.8.6 | SUGGESTED TUNES: FRANCONIA, ST. THOMAS

The advent of our God,
Our prayers must now employ,
And we must meet him on his road
With hymns of holy joy.

The everlasting Son,
Incarnate soon shall be:
He will a servant's form put on,
To make his people free.

Daughter of Zion, rise,
And greet thy lowly King,
And do not wickedly despise
The mercies he will bring.

As Judge, in clouds of light,
He will come down again,
And all his scattered saints unite
With him in heaven to reign.

Before that dreadful day,
May all our sin be gone;
May the old man be put away,
And the new man put on!

Praise to the Saviour-Son
From all the angel host;
Like praise be to the Father done,
And to the Holy Ghost.

THE LINDEN TREE CAROL

The carols that come to us from medieval times are often creative in their approach to the biblical stories. This carol is a case in point as it imagines the announcement to Mary (LUKE 1:26-38) *from the perspective of the angels. It is believed to date from the 15th century, and some of the English it uses is archaic.*

SHEET MUSIC FOR CHORAL SETTINGS CAN BE FOUND ONLINE

There stood in heaven a linden tree;
But, though 'twas honey-laden,
All angels cried, "No bloom shall be
Like that of one fair maiden."

Sped Gabriel on wingèd feet,
And passed through bolted portals,
In Nazareth, a maid to greet,
Blest o'er all other mortals.

"Hail Mary!" quod that angel mild,
"Of woman-kind the fairest:
The virgin, aye, shalt thou be styled,
A babe although thou bearest."

"How shall I bear a child, that ne'er
With wedded man was mated?
Pray tell me now this infant yhow
Shall he be generated?"

"O virgin sheen, it shall be seen,
As I announce afore thee:
The Holy Ghost, of virtue most,
Shall cast his shadow o'er thee."

"So be it!" God's handmaiden cried,
"According to thy telling."
Whereon the angel smartly hied
Up homeward to his dwelling.

This tiding filled his mates with glee:
'Twas passed from one to other,
That 'twas Marie, and none but she,
And God would call her mother.

THE LORD WILL COME AND NOT BE SLOW

Written by John Milton in the 17th century, this hymn paraphrases Psalms 85 and 86, which are traditionally associated with the season of Advent. Milton is best remembered for his epic poem "Paradise Lost."

METRE: 8.6.8.6 | SUGGESTED TUNES: ST. MAGNUS, ST. STEPHEN

The Lord will come and not be slow,
His footsteps cannot err;
Before him righteousness shall go,
His royal harbinger.
Truth from the earth, like to a flower,
Shall bud and blossom then;
And justice, from her heavenly bower,
Look down on mortal men.

Surely to such as do him fear,
Salvation is at hand!
And glory shall ere long appear
To dwell within our land.
Rise, God, judge thou the earth in might,
This wicked earth redress;
For thou art he who shalt by right
The nations all possess.

The nations all, whom thou hast made,
Shall come, and all shall frame,
To bow them low before thee, Lord,
And glorify thy Name.
For great thou art, and wonders great,

By thy strong hand are done:
Thou in thy everlasting seat
Remainest God alone.

THE TRUTH SENT FROM ABOVE (HEREFORDSHIRE CAROL)

This English folk carol was "collected" in the early 1900s, but dates from a much earlier period. It is usually sung with only a selection of the sixteen verses; for example, during Advent only the first five verses might be included.

METRE: 8.8.8.8 | SUGGESTED TUNE: THE TRUTH FROM ABOVE

This is the truth sent from above,
The truth of God, the God of love;
Therefore don't turn me from your door,
But hearken all, both rich and poor.

The first thing that I will relate,
That God at first did man create;
The next thing which to you I tell,
Woman was made with him to dwell.

Then after that, 'twas God's own choice,
To place them both in paradise,
There to remain from evil free,
Except they ate of such a tree.

But they did eat, which was a sin,
And then their ruin did begin—
Ruined themselves, both you and me,
And all of our posterity.

Thus we were heirs to endless woes,
Till God the Lord did interpose,
For so a promise soon did run,
That he'd redeem us with a Son.

And at this season of the year,
Our blest Redeemer did appear,
And here did live, and here did preach,
And many thousands he did teach.

Thus he in love to us behaved,
To show us how we might be saved,
And if you want to know the way,
Be pleased to hear what he did say.

"Go preach the gospel now," he said,
"To all the nations that are made,
And he that does believe on me,
From all his sins I'll set him free."

"If he believes and does obey,
I'll raise him up at the last day,
And now as sure as he does live,
Eternal life to him I'll give."

"But he that won't believe in me,
Eternal life shall never see,
If he will still in sin remain,
I'll give him everlasting pain."

"Now prove yourselves," the Teacher saith,
"Examine if you've any faith,
And if you search and can't this see,
Then beg of God to give it thee."

For he is merciful and kind,
And bids you seek and you shall find,
Your danger's great, make no delay,
For without faith you can't him see.

O seek it now while life does last,
For death is coming very fast,
And if he finds thee void of this,
The wrath of God you cannot miss.

O seek! O seek of God above,
That saving faith that works by love,
And if he's pleased to grant thee this,
Thou'rt sure to have eternal bliss.

For when by death he'll close thy eyes,
To be with Christ above the skies,
And there remain forever blessed,
With joys that cannot be expressed.

God grant to all within this place
True saving faith—that special grace,
Which to his people doth belong—
And thus I close my Christmas song.

"THY KINGDOM COME," ON BENDED KNEE

Written by American hymn writer Frederick Lucian Hosmer in 1891, this hymn expresses our longing for the second coming of Christ.

METRE: 8.6.8.6 | SUGGESTED TUNES: IRISH, ST. FLAVIAN

"Thy kingdom come," on bended knee,
The passing ages pray;
And faithful souls have yearned to see
On earth that kingdom's day.

But the slow watches of the night
Not less to God belong,
And for the everlasting right
The silent stars are strong.

And lo, already on the hills
The flags of dawn appear;
Gird up your loins, ye prophet souls,
Proclaim the day is near:

The day in whose clear-shining light

All wrong shall stand revealed,
When justice shall be throned in might,
And every hurt be healed:

When knowledge, hand in hand with peace,
Shall walk the earth abroad—
The day of perfect righteousness,
The promised day of God.

TOMORROW SHALL BE MY DANCING DAY

This carol is believed to have originated in the 14th century, and like many medieval carols, it has an extensive number of verses, most of which are usually omitted today. The words review the gospel story through the lens of Christ's love for his bride.

SHEET MUSIC FOR A VARIETY OF CHORAL SETTINGS CAN BE FOUND ONLINE (RECOMMENDED: JOHN RUTTER)

Tomorrow shall be my dancing day;
I would my true love did so chance
To see the legend of my play;
To call my true love to my dance.

Sing, oh my love! Oh my love, my love, my love!
This have I done for my true love.

Then was I born of a virgin pure,
Of her I took fleshly substance;
Thus was I knit to man's nature,
To call my true love to my dance.

Sing, oh my love! Oh my love, my love, my love!
This have I done for my true love.

In a manger laid, and wrapped I was;
So very poor, this was my chance,
Betwixt an ox and a silly poor ass,

To call my true love to my dance.

Sing, oh my love! Oh my love, my love, my love!
This have I done for my true love.

Then afterwards baptised I was;
The Holy Ghost on me did glance,
My Father's voice heard I from above,
To call my true love to my dance.

Sing, oh my love! Oh my love, my love, my love!
This have I done for my true love.

Into the desert I was led,
Where I fasted without substance;
The devil bade me make stones my bread,
To have me break my true love's dance.

Sing, oh my love! Oh my love, my love, my love!
This have I done for my true love.

For thirty pence, Judas me sold,
His covetousness for to advance:
Mark whom I kiss, the same do hold!
The same is he shall lead the dance.

Sing, oh my love! Oh my love, my love, my love!
This have I done for my true love.

Before Pilate, the Jews me brought,
Where Barabbas had deliverance;
They scourged me and set me at nought,
Judged me to die to lead the dance.

Sing, oh my love! Oh my love, my love, my love!
This have I done for my true love.

Then on the cross hanged I was,
Where a spear my heart did glance;
There issued forth both water and blood,
To call my true love to my dance.

Sing, oh my love! Oh my love, my love, my love!
This have I done for my true love.

Then down to hell I took my way,
For my true love's deliverance,
And rose again on the third day,
Up to my true love and the dance.

Sing, oh my love! Oh my love, my love, my love!
This have I done for my true love.

Then up to heaven I did ascend,
Where now I dwell in sure substance,
On the right hand of God, that man
May come unto the general dance.

Sing, oh my love! Oh my love, my love, my love!
This have I done for my true love.

WAKE, O WAKE! WITH TIDINGS THRILLING (WACHET AUF, RUFT UNS DIE STIMME)

Written in German in the late 16th century by Philipp Nicolai, and translated into English in the early 1900s by Francis Crawford Burkitt, this hymn is inspired by the eschatological parable of the patient virgins (MATTHEW 25:1-13).

METRE IS IRREGULAR | TUNE: WACHET AUF

Wake, O wake! With tidings thrilling,
The watchmen all the air are filling,
Arise, Jerusalem, arise!
Midnight strikes! No more delaying,
"The hour has come!" we hear them saying,
"Where are ye all, ye virgins wise?
The Bridegroom comes in sight,

Raise high your torches bright!"
Alleluia! The wedding song swells loud and strong:
Go forth and join the festal throng.

Zion hears the watchmen shouting,
Her heart leaps up with joy undoubting,
She stands and waits with eager eyes;
See her friend from heaven descending,
Adorned with truth and grace unending!
Her light burns clear, her star doth rise.
Now come, thou precious crown,
Lord Jesus, God's own Son!
Alleluia! Let us prepare to follow there,
Where in thy supper we may share.

Every soul in thee rejoices;
From earth and from angelic voices,
Be glory given to thee alone!
Now the gates of pearl receive us,
Thy presence never more shall leave us,
We stand with angels round thy throne.
Earth cannot give below,
The bliss thou dost bestow.
Alleluia! Grant us to raise, to length of days,
The triumph-chorus of thy praise.

RESOURCE NO. 5

The O Antiphons

The O Antiphons are the liturgical antecedent of the still-popular hymn "O Come, O Come, Emmanuel." Originating in the monasteries of 6th century Italy, the antiphons are a set of seven sung prayers designed to be recited at the service of Evening Prayer during the last week before Christmas—to be repeated before and after the Magnificat (MARY'S SONG IN LUKE 1:46-55). Each of these prayers begins with a title for Jesus, and is followed by a reflection and petition, forming a brief meditation upon the promised Messiah.

The schedule for the antiphons looks like this:

December 17: O Sapientia (O Wisdom)
December 18: O Adonai (O Lord)
December 19: O Radix Jesse (O Root of Jesse)
December 20: O Clavis David (O Key of David)
December 21: O Oriens (O Dayspring)
December 22: O Rex Gentium (O King of the Nations)
December 23: O Emmanuel (O God With Us)

You'll notice that the original titles were in Latin. What is less noticeable, but nonetheless meaningful, is that the titles in Latin form a "reverse acrostic" spelling the Latin phrase "Ero Cras" which translates roughly as "Tomorrow I shall be there." This hidden phrase refers both to the immanence of the celebration of Christmas, as well as the expectation of Christ's second coming.

It should also be noted that in some traditions there is an eighth antiphon which, when observed, pushes the start date for the antiphons back a day to the 16th of December. This eighth antiphon celebrates Mary's role in the incarnation and is called "O Virgin of Virgins" (O Virgo virginum). It's clear, however, that this was not a part of the original set, as it does not fit into the acrostic.

The O Antiphons were paraphrased into hymn format in the 8th or

9th century. It was not until the mid 1800s that the hymn "Veni, veni, Emmanuel," was translated into English and popularised by John Mason Neale.

Included below are English translations of the ancient antiphons themselves, alongside the corresponding verses from the hymn which they inspired.

DECEMBER 17: O SAPIENTIA (O WISDOM)

ANTIPHON:

O Wisdom, coming forth from the mouth of the Most High, reaching from one end of the heavens to the other, mightily and sweetly ordering all things: Come and teach us the way of prudence.

HYMN:

O come, thou Wisdom from on high,
And order all things, far and nigh;
To us the path of knowledge show,
And cause us in her ways to go.
Rejoice! Rejoice! Emmanuel
Shall come to thee, O Israel.

DECEMBER 18: O ADONAI (O LORD)

ANTIPHON:

O Lord, and Ruler of the House of Israel, who appeared unto Moses in the flame of a burning bush, and gavest to him the Law on Sinai: Come and redeem us with an outstretched arm.

HYMN:

O come, Adonai, Lord of might,
Who to thy tribes, on Sinai's height,
In ancient times didst give the law,
In cloud and majesty and awe.
Rejoice! Rejoice! Emmanuel
Shall come to thee, O Israel.

DECEMBER 19: O RADIX JESSE (O ROOT OF JESSE)

ANTIPHON:

O Root of Jesse, which stands for an ensign of the people, before whom the kings keep silence and unto whom the Gentiles shall make supplication: Come to deliver us, and tarry not.

HYMN:

O come, thou Rod of Jesse, free
Thine own from Satan's tyranny;
From depths of hell thy people save,
And give them victory o'er the grave.
Rejoice! Rejoice! Emmanuel
Shall come to thee, O Israel.

DECEMBER 20: O CLAVIS DAVID (O KEY OF DAVID)

ANTIPHON:

O Key of David and Sceptre of the House of Israel, who openest and none shutteth, who shuttest and none openeth: Come thou, and bring forth the captive from the house of bondage, who sitteth in darkness and in the shadow of death.

HYMN:

O come, thou Key of David, come
And open wide our heav'nly home;
Make safe the way that leads on high,
And close the path to misery.
Rejoice! Rejoice! Emmanuel
Shall come to thee, O Israel.

DECEMBER 21: O ORIENS (O DAYSPRING)

ANTIPHON:

O Dayspring, Splendour of Light Eternal and Sun of Righteousness: Come and give light to those who dwell in darkness and the shadow of death.

HYMN:

O come, thou Dayspring, from on high,
And cheer us by thy drawing nigh;
Disperse the gloomy clouds of night,
And death's dark shadows put to flight.
Rejoice! Rejoice! Emmanuel
Shall come to thee, O Israel.

DECEMBER 22: O REX GENTIUM (O KING OF THE NATIONS)

ANTIPHON:

O King of the Nations and their Desire, thou Cornerstone that dost make both one: Come and deliver man, whom thou didst form out of the dust of the earth.

HYMN:

O come, Desire of nations, bind
All peoples in one heart and mind;
Bid envy, strife and quarrels cease;
Fill the whole world with heaven's peace.
Rejoice! Rejoice! Emmanuel
Shall come to thee, O Israel.

DECEMBER 23: O EMMANUEL (O GOD WITH US)

ANTIPHON:

O Emmanuel, our King and Lawgiver, the Hope of the Nations and their Saviour: Come thou to save us, O Lord our God.

HYMN:

O come, O come, Emmanuel,
And ransom captive Israel,
That mourns in lonely exile here,
Until the Son of God appear.
Rejoice! Rejoice! Emmanuel
Shall come to thee, O Israel.

RESOURCE NO. 6

Nine Lessons & Carols

This beloved Christmas Eve liturgy is believed to have originated at Truro Cathedral (Cornwall, UK) in the late nineteenth century. It was later popularised by King's College, Cambridge (UK)—where it is still offered annually in grand fashion.

The structure of the service is quite simple. It is comprised of a series of scripture readings interspersed with music, some of which may be sung by a choir and some of which may be sung congregationally. The service is reminiscent of the (much older) traditional Easter Vigil liturgy, which traces the roots of the Christian salvation-story through a series of scripture readings, transitioning from the solemnity of Lent to the jubilant celebration of the resurrection. In the same way, it is through the review of these scripture "lessons" that participants in this Christmas Eve tradition are reminded of the "backstory" to the miracle of the incarnation.

Because this service marks the point where Advent flows into Christmas, it is appropriate to include both Advent and Christmas music. Traditionally, one or two songs are sung between each reading and the selections often change from year to year, though it is customary for the service to begin with "Once in Royal David's City" and to conclude with "O Come, All Ye Faithful." Included in the resource below are suggestions for hymns and carols. (Commonly performed carols which are not in English or which are distracting in theological emphasis have been omitted.)

It is the custom at King's College, Cambridge for the lessons to be read by a range of individuals serving in different capacities—from a child in the choir to the head of the college. In a congregational setting, a similar model could be followed, ensuring that a wide range of participants are included—both lay people who serve in less visible ways, as well as ordained members of the clergy. You will notice that the readings are traditionally done in the King James Version, as included be-

low, though some congregations may prefer to use a modern-language translation.

PROCESSIONAL HYMN

Once in Royal David's City

OPENING ADDRESS & PRAYER:

Beloved in Christ: Be it this Christmas Eve our care and delight to prepare ourselves to hear again the message of the angels; in heart and mind to go even unto Bethlehem and see this thing which is come to pass, and the babe lying in a manger.

Let us read and mark in holy scripture the tale of the loving purposes of God from the first days of our disobedience unto the glorious redemption brought us by this holy child; and let us make this place glad with our carols of praise.

But first, let us pray for the needs of his whole world; for peace and health over all the earth; for unity and goodwill within the Church he came to build; and because this of all things would rejoice his heart, let us at this time remember in his name the poor and the helpless, the cold and the hungry, the abused, the exploited and the oppressed; the sick in body and in mind and them that mourn; the isolated, the lonely and the unloved; the elderly and the little children; all who know not the Lord Jesus, or who love him not, or who by sin have grieved his heart of love.

Lastly, let us remember before God all those who rejoice with us, but upon another shore and in a greater light, that multitude which no man can number, whose hope was in the Word made flesh, and with whom, in this Lord Jesus, we for evermore are one.

These prayers and praises let us humbly offer up to the throne of heaven, in the words which Christ himself hath taught us:

> *Our Father, who art in heaven, hallowed be thy name, thy kingdom come, thy will be done, on earth as it is in heaven. Give us this day our daily bread. And forgive us our trespasses, as we forgive them that trespass against us. And lead us not into temptation; but deliver us from evil. For thine is the kingdom, the power and the glory, for ever and ever. Amen.*

FIRST LESSON: GENESIS 3:8-19

God tells sinful Adam that he has lost the life of paradise and that his seed will bruise the serpent's head.

And they heard the voice of the LORD God walking in the garden in the cool of the day: and Adam and his wife hid themselves from the presence of the LORD God amongst the trees of the garden. And the LORD God called unto Adam, and said unto him, Where art thou? And he said, I heard thy voice in the garden, and I was afraid, because I was naked; and I hid myself. And he said, Who told thee that thou wast naked? Hast thou eaten of the tree, whereof I commanded thee that thou shouldest not eat? And the man said, The woman whom thou gavest to be with me, she gave me of the tree, and I did eat. And the LORD God said unto the woman, What is this that thou hast done? And the woman said, The serpent beguiled me, and I did eat. And the LORD God said unto the serpent, Because thou hast done this, thou art cursed above all cattle, and above every beast of the field. Upon thy belly shalt thou go, and dust shalt thou eat all the days of thy life: and I will put enmity between thee and the woman, and between thy seed and her seed; it shall bruise thy head, and thou shalt bruise his heel. Unto the woman he said, I will greatly multiply thy sorrow and thy conception; in sorrow thou shalt bring forth children; and thy desire shall be to thy husband, and he shall rule over thee. And unto Adam he said, Because thou hast hearkened unto the voice of thy wife, and hast eaten of the tree, of which I commanded thee, saying, Thou shalt not eat of it: cursed is the ground for thy sake; in sorrow shalt thou eat of it all the days of thy life; thorns also and thistles shall it bring forth to thee; and thou shalt eat the herb of the field; in the sweat of thy face shalt thou eat bread, till thou return unto the ground; for out of it wast thou taken: for dust thou art, and unto dust shalt thou return.

SUGGESTED CAROLS

The Truth Sent From Above
Come, Thou Long Expected Jesus
Jesu, Joy of Man's Desiring

SECOND LESSON: GENESIS 22:15-18

God promises to faithful Abraham that in his seed shall all the nations of the earth be blessed.

And the angel of the Lord called unto Abraham out of heaven the second time, and said, By myself have I sworn, saith the Lord, for because thou hast done this thing, and hast not withheld thy son, thine only son: that in blessing I will bless thee, and in multiplying I will multiply thy seed as the stars of the heaven, and as the sand which is upon the sea shore; and thy seed shall possess the gate of his enemies; and in thy seed shall all the nations of the earth be blessed; because thou hast obeyed my voice.

SUGGESTED CAROLS

Come, Thou Redeemer of the Earth
O Come, O Come, Emmanuel
O Come, Divine Messiah

THIRD LESSON: ISAIAH 9:2,6-7

The prophet foretells the coming of the Saviour.

The people that walked in darkness have seen a great light; they that dwell in the land of the shadow of death, upon them hath the light shined...

For unto us a child is born, unto us a son is given: and the government shall be upon his shoulder; and his name shall be called Wonderful, Counsellor, The Mighty God, The Everlasting Father, The Prince of Peace.

Of the increase of his government and peace there shall be no end, upon the throne of David, and upon his kingdom, to order it, and to establish it with judgment and with justice from henceforth even forever. The zeal of the LORD of hosts will perform this.

SUGGESTED CAROLS

O Little Town of Bethlehem
Creator of the Stars of Night
Lo, How A Rose E'er Blooming

FOURTH LESSON: ISAIAH 11:1-9

The peace that Christ will bring is foreshown.

And there shall come forth a rod out of the stem of Jesse, and a Branch shall grow out of his roots: and the spirit of the LORD shall rest upon him, the spirit of wisdom and understanding, the spirit of counsel and might, the spirit of knowledge and of the fear of the LORD; and shall make him of quick understanding in the fear of the LORD.

And he shall not judge after the sight of his eyes, neither reprove after the hearing of his ears; but with righteousness shall he judge the poor, and reprove with equity for the meek of the earth; and he shall smite the earth with the rod of his mouth, and with the breath of his lips shall he slay the wicked. And righteousness shall be the girdle of his loins, and faithfulness the girdle of his reins.

The wolf also shall dwell with the lamb, and the leopard shall lie down with the kid; and the calf and the young lion and the fatling together; and a little child shall lead them. And the cow and the bear shall feed; their young ones shall lie down together: and the lion shall eat straw like the ox. And the sucking child shall play on the hole of the asp, and the weaned child shall put his hand on the cockatrice' den. They shall not hurt nor destroy in all my holy mountain: for the earth shall be full of the knowledge of the LORD, as the waters cover the sea.

SUGGESTED CAROLS

Gabriel's Message
Of the Father's Love Begotten
The Holly and the Ivy

FIFTH LESSON: LUKE 1:26-35,38

The angel Gabriel salutes the blessed virgin Mary.

And in the sixth month the angel Gabriel was sent from God unto a city of Galilee named Nazareth, to a virgin espoused to a man whose name was Joseph of the house of David; and the virgin's name was Mary. And the angel came in unto her and said, Hail, thou that art highly favoured, the Lord is with thee: blessed art thou among women. And when she saw him, she was troubled at his saying, and cast in her mind what manner of salutation this should be. And the angel said unto her, Fear not, Mary: for thou hast found favour with God. And, behold, thou shalt conceive in thy womb, and bring forth a son, and shalt call his name JESUS. He shall be great, and shall be called the Son of the Highest: and the Lord God shall give unto him the throne of his father David; and he shall reign over the house of Jacob forever; and of his kingdom there shall be no end.

Then said Mary unto the angel, How shall this be, seeing I know not a man? And the angel answered and said unto her, The Holy Ghost shall come upon thee, and the power of the Highest shall overshadow thee: therefore also that holy thing which shall be born of thee shall be called the Son of God.

SUGGESTED CAROLS

Good Christian Men, Rejoice
God Rest Ye Merry, Gentlemen
What Child is This?

SIXTH LESSON: LUKE 2:1,3-7

Saint Luke tells of the birth of Jesus.

And it came to pass in those days, that there went out a decree from Caesar Augustus, that all the world should be taxed. And all went to be taxed, everyone into his own city. And Joseph also went up from Galilee, out of the city of Nazareth, into Judea, unto the city of David, which is called Bethlehem; (because he was of the house and lineage of David:) to be taxed with Mary his espoused wife, being great with child.

And so it was, that while they were there, the days were accomplished that she should be delivered. And she brought forth her firstborn son, and wrapped him in swaddling clothes, and laid him in a manger; because there was no room for them in the inn.

SUGGESTED CAROLS

In the Bleak Midwinter
Angels, from the Realms of Glory
See, Amid the Winter's Snow
Hark! the Herald Angels Sing
Angels We Have Heard on High
It Came upon the Midnight Clear
The First Noel

LUKE 2:8-16

The shepherds go to the manger.

And there were in the same country shepherds abiding in the field, keeping watch over their flock by night. And, lo, the angel of the Lord came upon them, and the glory of the Lord shone round about them: and they were sore afraid. And the angel said unto them, Fear not: for, behold, I bring you good tidings of great joy, which shall be to all people. For unto you is born this day in the city of David a Saviour, which is Christ the Lord. And this shall be a sign unto you; Ye shall find the babe wrapped in swaddling clothes, and lying in a manger. And suddenly there was with the angel a multitude of the heavenly host praising God, and saying, Glory to God in the highest, and on earth peace, goodwill toward men.

And it came to pass, as the angels were gone away from them into heaven, the shepherds said one to another, Let us now go even unto Bethlehem, and see this thing which is come to pass, which the Lord hath made known unto us. And they came with haste, and found Mary, and Joseph, and the babe lying in a manger.

SUGGESTED CAROLS

Silent Night, Holy Night
While Shepherds Watched Their Flocks by Night
We Three Kings
As With Gladness Men of Old
Brightest and Best of the Sons of the Morning
O Worship the Lord in the Beauty of Holiness

SEVENTH LESSON: MATTHEW 2:1-12

The wise men are led by the star to Jesus.

Now when Jesus was born in Bethlehem of Judea in the days of Herod the king, behold, there came wise men from the east to Jerusalem, saying, Where is he that is born King of the Jews? For we have seen his star in the east, and are come to worship him. When Herod the king had heard these things, he was troubled, and all Jerusalem with him. And when he had gathered all the chief priests and scribes of the people together, he demanded of them where Christ should be born. And they said unto him, In Bethlehem of Judea: for thus it is written by the prophet, And thou Bethlehem, in the land of Judah, art not the least among the princes of Judah: for out of thee shall come a Governor, that shall rule my people Israel.

Then Herod, when he had privily called the wise men, enquired of them diligently what time the star appeared.

And he sent them to Bethlehem, and said, Go and search diligently for the young child; and when ye have found him, bring me word again, that I may come and worship him also.

When they had heard the king, they departed; and, lo, the star, which they saw in the east, went before them till it came and stood over where the young child was. When they saw the star, they rejoiced with exceeding great joy. And when they were come into the house, they saw the young child with Mary his mother, and fell down, and worshipped him. And when they had opened their treasures, they presented unto him gifts: gold and frankincense and myrrh. And being warned of God in a dream that they should not return to Herod, they departed into their own country another way.

SUGGESTED CAROLS

Joy to the World
I Heard the Bells on Christmas Day
From East to West, From Shore to Shore
Christians Awake! Salute the Happy Morn
I Saw Three Ships
Go Tell It on the Mountain

NINTH LESSON: JOHN 1:1-14

Saint John unfolds the great mystery of the Incarnation.

In the beginning was the Word, and the Word was with God, and the Word was God. The same was in the beginning with God. All things were made by him; and without him was not anything made that was made. In him was life; and the life was the light of men. And the light shineth in darkness; and the darkness comprehended it not.

There was a man sent from God, whose name was John. The same came for a witness, to bear witness of the Light, that all men through him might believe. He was not that Light, but was sent to bear witness of that Light. That was the true Light, which lighteth every man that cometh into the world. He was in the world, and the world was made by him, and the world knew him not. He came unto his own, and his own received him not. But as many as received him, to them he gave power to become the sons of God, even to them that believe on his name: which were born, not of blood, nor of the will of the flesh, nor of the will of man, but of God. And the Word was made flesh, and dwelt among us, (and we beheld his glory, the glory as of the only begotten of the Father), full of grace and truth.

CLOSING HYMN

O Come, All Ye Faithful

COLLECT FOR CHRISTMAS

O God, who makest us glad with the yearly remembrance of the birth of thy only son, Jesus Christ: Grant that as we joyfully receive him for our Redeemer, so we may with sure confidence behold him, when he shall come to be our Judge; who liveth and reigneth with thee and the Holy Spirit, one God, world without end. *Amen.*

DISMISSAL BLESSING

May Christ, who by his incarnation gathered into one things earthly and heavenly, fill you with joy and peace; and the blessing of God Almighty, the Father, the Son and the Holy Spirit, be amongst you and remain with you always. *Amen.*

Acknowledgements

My first experience of liturgical worship was during Bible college, and it shocked me. I had an Evangelical's distrust of pomp, ceremony, and ritual. Nothing had prepared me for the depth and richness I would discover in the worship of a little Anglican parish that had done its best to preserve a centuries-old form of worship. The lengthy service, its hymns, responses, prayers and readings were all packed with scripture. Every phrase of the ancient liturgy was an invitation to contemplation. Most of the service involved congregational participation in some form. There was a reverent spirit throughout, wonderfully long silences were left for private prayer, and all of my senses were engaged and focused. My definition of a "worshipful" service was challenged and transformed. This was not at all the dull and meaningless routine that I'd expected it to be! Now, were there serious flaws to be found in the setting to which I refer? Undeniably. But there were also spiritual riches beyond price. Parishes like this one were the keepers of an ancient Christian tradition that I had been missing, longing for, even without knowing it.

This is how I came to discover many of the texts that are woven into the pages of this book. But to tell you about my "liturgical awakening" is really to bring you in at the middle of the story. Without a strong personal faith in Jesus Christ—nurtured by the example of faithful men and women, rooted in holy scripture and supported by the fellowship of believers—I might have lacked the crucial foundation which alone can give life and meaning to these devotional practices.

So, with that said, I must first acknowledge a debt to the people in my life who were instrumental in my coming to faith, who have inspired me with their examples of study and devotion, and who have been my companions on the journey. In particular, I want to acknowledge my parents, who continue to be among the greatest blessings of my life.

I also owe an immense debt of gratitude to those churches where I have had the joy and privilege of experiencing these living ancient traditions. I've been blessed to know and benefit from the scholarship of faithful priests, pastors, monks, and nuns. Moreover, the generosity and humility of sextons, sacristans, and other oft-overlooked servers and laypeople has not only satisfied my ecclesiastical curiosity, but inspired my spirit. I hope that I have managed to do justice to what I've learned from them in this book, and to share these gifts of the Advent season in a way that enriches many more believers.

Finally, I want to take a moment to thank the friends and family who encouraged me, challenged me, and provided crucial editorial feedback during the writing of the manuscript: I love you and I'm so grateful for you.

- Kerry van der Vinne

AMBRY
PRESS

ambrypress.com

Made in the USA
Columbia, SC
24 October 2023

24861907R00096